Loving One Another

GENE A. GETZ

While this book is designed for the reader's personal enjoyment and profit, it is also intended for group study. A leader's guide is available from your local Christian bookstore or from the publisher.

VICTOR BOOKS

a division of SP Publications, Inc.

WHEATON ILLINOIS 60187

Offices also in Fullerton, California • Whitby, Ontario, Canada • Amersham-on-the-Hill, Bucks, England

Third printing, 1981

Recommended Dewey Decimal Classification: 260
  Suggested Subject Headings: Church; Christianity

Library of Congress Catalog Card Number: 79-63540
ISBN: 0-88207-786-4

© 1979 by SP Publications, Inc. All rights reserved
Printed in the United States of America

VICTOR BOOKS
A division of SP Publications, Inc.
P.O. Box 1825 · Wheaton, Illinois 60187

Contents

Preface

This is a book on evangelism. You might think it should begin where most studies on evangelism and missions begin—with the Great Commission in Matthew 28:19-20. There Christ said to His followers, just before He returned to heaven, to "go and make disciples of all nations."

Actually, this is not where evangelism began in the New Testament. Christ's specific instructions to believers, regarding *how* to reach lost mankind with the good news of salvation, began at a point earlier in His earthly ministry. In fact, we cannot really understand the Great Commission as it is stated in Matthew 28:19-20 unless we understand its larger context.

Christ's command to "make disciples" involves a much larger perspective than we often realize, not only biblically but conceptually. The larger context *biblically* began in the Upper Room in John 13 and the larger context *conceptually* begins with Christians who love one another as Christ loved them. Without this enlarged viewpoint we cannot comprehend the evangelistic nature of the letters that were written to the New Testament churches. In fact, we will tend to conclude that their purpose was solely for edification and will miss their evangelistic thrust altogether.

Church groups that begin with Matthew 28:19-20 as a point of departure for developing their evangelistic strategy are usually in one of two categories. Some concentrate on *personal* evangelism, with an emphasis on sharing Christ, one on one. Others concentrate on *mass* evangelism with an emphasis on preaching and proclamation. While neither group excludes the other's approach, each has its dominant emphasis.

Unfortunately, both groups often overlook an important New Testament principle. God's plan is that local bodies of believers, functioning as loving and caring units, provide a dynamic

4

community in which both personal witnessing and evangelistic preaching can become intensely productive. Furthermore, when local churches begin to function as God intended, cooperative evengelistic ventures will also reap much greater results.

This is what this book is about. My goal has been to present the total New Testament perspective on the subject of evangelism, also including the "evangelistic" aspects of the Old Testament that help us to understand the New.

Gene A. Getz

Acknowledgement

I want to express my appreciation to the members of the body of Christ—both at Fellowship Bible Church of Park Cities and Fellowship Bible Church in North Dallas, where I first developed and presented this material. I'm indeed thankful for Christians who seek to exemplify the concepts in this book—not as we should, of course, but as a goal for our lives together as members of the family of God.

I also want to acknowledge three men who carefully read and evaluated this material and offered helpful suggestions: Barry Applewhite, fellow pastor at Fellowship Bible Church, with whom I have the privilege of sharing the primary teaching ministry; Mike Cocoris, part-time professor at Dallas Theological Seminary and vice president of EvanTell, a unique Bible teaching/evangelistic ministry; and Dr. Ed Blum, assistant professor of systematic theology at Dallas Theological Seminary. Thanks, men, for your time, effort, and encouragement.

Thanks too to the editorial staff of Victor Books. I found them to be dedicated in their task, exacting in their work, and sensitive to me—an author.

A new commandment I give you: love one another.
John 13:34a

1

A New Commandment

One day I picked up a copy of a book written by Dr. Francis Schaeffer entitled *The Mark of the Christian*. Few books have touched my life like this one. Once I began reading, I couldn't put it down.

The book contained a very simple exposition of Christ's words to His disciples, as recorded by John: "A new commandment I give you," said Jesus. "Love one another. As I have loved you, so you must love one another." Then Christ added the bottom line, the primary purpose for this new commandment. "All men will know that you are My disciples if you love one another" (John 13:34-35).

I began to see that the Great Commission to reach the world with the Gospel did not begin with Christ's final words to His followers in Matthew 28:19-20. Rather, it began with His words to the disciples in the Upper Room, prior to His death. It was at the Last Supper that Jesus began laying down a profound plan for reaching all men with the truth of who He was and why He had come into this world.

At that moment Christ made three important statements to these men:

- **"A new commandment I give you: love one another."**
- **"As I have loved you, so you must love one another."**

* **"All men will know that you are My disciples if you love one another."**

Christ's basic concern in each of these three statements stands out boldly—love for one another. But each statement also contains a unique concept. First, to love one another was a *new commandment*. Second, Christ's love for them was to be their *model* in loving one another. And third, this love was to be the *means* whereby the apostles could communicate to all men the One whom they were emulating in their relationships.

Let's focus on Christ's first statement. Why was this a new commandment? How does this new commandment relate to the old commandment? How do both the old and the new relate to our task to bring people to Christ?

The Immediate Context

For nearly three-and-one-half years Jesus had engaged in a public ministry. He had taught people who He was, verifying His deity with miraculous signs. Because of His teachings and His miracles, He experienced a growing popularity among the masses, culminating in His triumphal entry into Jerusalem (John 12:12-16). He also experienced a growing hatred from the religious leaders. They were desperately threatened, not only by His words that judged their hypocrisy, but also by the growing number of people who were attracted to Him and His teachings (12:17-19).

In His own heart, "Jesus knew that the time had come for Him to leave this world and go to the Father" (13:1). Consequently, He withdrew from His public ministry and met privately with the Twelve to prepare them in a special way for the events that lay just ahead—His betrayal and death, His resurrection and ascension. It was in the Upper Room, while having a meal with His men, that He commanded them to love one another (John 13:34-35).

When Christ said, "A new commandment I give you," He was obviously making a comparison that was both a contrast and an extension of truth. It was a contrast in that Christ was telling them about a new way to make people aware of their sins and to bring them to Christ. It was an extension of truth because it involved the fulfillment of a promise God had made many, many years before, both to Adam and Abraham.

The Old Commandment

When we hear the word *commandment*, we usually think of God's Law, given to Israel at Mount Sinai and recorded in Exodus, Leviticus, Numbers, and Deuteronomy. But sometimes the whole Old Testament is referred to as God's Law (see Matt. 22:40 and John 12:34). In any case, the very foundation of this Law is the Ten Commandments, recorded in Exodus 20 and Deuteronomy 5. The numerous other laws, statutes, and commandments God revealed to Moses were an elaboration and application of the Ten.

Why was the Law (the old commandment) given? Unfortunately, many people believe it was so that they—by keeping the commandments—may inherit eternal life. Not so! "No one will be declared righteous in His [God's] sight by observing the Law," wrote Paul to the Romans (Rom. 3:20). To the Galatians he wrote just as emphatically, "Clearly no one is justified before God by the Law" (Gal. 3:11).

It is impossible for any human being to keep the Law perfectly. If you fail in any respect, you have fallen short of God's standard and cannot be saved (Rom. 3:23). As Paul stated further, "Cursed is everyone who does not continue to do everything written in the book of the Law" (Gal. 3:10).

Since God knew this before He ever revealed His Law to Moses, why then did He give the Law? If no one can keep the Law perfectly, why would the Lord impose these commandments on us?

Paul answered these questions clearly in his Letter to the Galatians. **"The Law was put in charge to lead us to Christ that we might be jusitified by faith"** (Gal. 3:24). Here Paul used a metaphor to illustrate an important truth regarding our salvation. The New American Standard Bible makes it even more obvious: "Therefore the Law has become our tutor to lead us to Christ, that we may be justified by faith."

The Greek word translated "tutor" is *paidagogos*. It literally refers to a guide and guardian of young boys. This man was usually a slave who made sure the young person in his charge got to school regularly and on time. When the boy was not under the schoolmaster's supervision, the paidagogos (tutor) was responsible to make sure he conducted himself properly.

In other words, the tutor was a disciplinarian. Sometimes he was harsh and cruel, as illustrated in ancient art. The paidagogos was often pictured as a man with a rod in his hand ready to strike a disobedient boy.

The paidagogos, wrote Paul, illustrates the nature of the Law and why God gave it. The Law was our tutor, our disciplinarian, that brought us to Christ. Christ is represented in the metaphor not by the paidagogos or tutor but by the schoolmaster. Once we are in "school," that is, in Christ and under His guidance, we are free from the paidagogos, the Law.

This same word, paidagogos, is translated "schoolmaster" in the King James Version. Unfortunately, this causes the reader to miss the real meaning of Paul's metaphor.

Thus Paul wrote, "Now that faith has come [faith in Christ], we are no longer under the supervision of the Law" (Gal. 3:25). We "are all sons of God through faith in Christ Jesus" (3:26).

Just prior to this tutor illustration, Paul used another metaphor to describe the Law's purpose. When people break the law in our society, they are often put behind bars—in prison. Just so, Paul wrote, "Before this faith came [faith in Christ], we were held *prisoners* by the Law, locked up until faith should be revealed" (3:23).[1] In other words, since no one could keep the Law, we were all under sin's domination and control. We were all in captivity.

Paul illustrated this truth in his own life in his letter to the Roman Christians. "I would not have known what sin was except

---

[1] Hereafter, all italicized words in Scripture references are used for emphasis.

through the Law," he declared (Rom. 7:7). "But in order that sin [a reality that exists whether we know it or not] might be recognized as sin, it [the Law] produced death in me . . . so that through the commandment sin might become utterly sinful" (7:13).

In a sense, it was the Old Testament Law that led Paul to Christ. It was through the Law that he became "conscious of sin" and realized that he needed a Saviour from sin.

What about people who never know about God's Law? Paul was a Jew. He was aware of the Law through his religious heritage. What about those who were never exposed to the Law? What about the people who lived even before the Law was revealed at Mount Sinai?

These are very legitimate questions, particularly for a non-Jew. In fact, these questions were being asked by both Jews and Gentiles in the New Testament world. Consequently, Paul answered these questions: "For before the Law was given, sin was in the world. But sin is not taken into account [that is, by the lawbreaker] when there is no law. Nevertheless, death reigned from the time of Adam to the time of Moses, even over those who did not sin by breaking a command" (Rom. 5:13-14). This is why Paul had written earlier in his letter that "all have sinned and fall short of the glory of God" (3:23).

The Old Testament Law was given to make *all* people aware of their sins; to cause them to seek a way of escape; and to lead them to Christ. "The Law was added so that the trespass might increase. But where sin increased, grace increased all the more" (5:20). In other words, God made a way of escape through Jesus Christ.

The New Commandment

The Old Testament Law then was given to cause people to seek Jesus Christ. But once Christ came, He introduced a *new* commandment—a new means to lead people to God and to make them aware of sin and the answer for that sin. The *new* means was inherent in the *new* commandment to "love one another."

By this, He said, "All men will know you are My disciples."

Through Christian love and fellowship, we were drawn to Christ. Because He provides the power to free us from sin's grip, we are no longer condemned. God accepts us because of the work Christ completed at Calvary.

The world today is filled with religious systems that teach that we can be saved by doing good works. Many of these systems are offshoots of Christianity and invariably give their followers the impression that the only way they can be sure of eternal life is to keep the Old Testament Law, particularly the Ten Commandments. Obviously they have missed the whole point of the Law, for the Bible makes it very clear that no one can be saved in this way. Consider the following:

"All who rely on observing the Law are under a curse, for it is written: 'Cursed is everyone who does not continue to do everything written in the Book of the Law.' Clearly no one is justified before God by the Law, because, 'The righteous will live by faith.' The Law is not based on faith; on the contrary, 'The man who does these things will live by them.' Christ redeemed us from the curse of the Law by becoming a curse for us, for it is written: 'Cursed is everyone who is hung on a tree' " (Gal. 3:10-13).

There are also religious systems in the world that have no direct theological relationship to Christianity. However, these systems, though they do not utilize biblical laws, come up with their own systems of good works for achieving success in some future life. But the Bible clearly rejects any "works system" for attaining eternal life. Look at these two New Testament passages that emphasize the importance of faith:

"For it is by grace you have been saved, through faith—and this not from yourselves, it is the gift of God—not by works, so that no one can boast" (Eph. 2:8-9).

"Now when a man works, his wages are not credited to him as a gift, but as an obligation. However, to the man who does not work but trusts God who justifies the wicked, his faith is credited as righteousness" (Rom. 4:4-5).

A Personal Response

What about your life? Are you trying to achieve eternal life by obeying the Ten Commandments, by doing good, by "loving your neighbor"? Even the Old Testament teaches that, "All our righteous deeds are like a filthy garment" (Isa. 64:6). This does not mean that what you may be doing is not good in itself. However, even what is "good" is not good enough to give you eternal life.

It is only by faith in *Christ's* goodness and righteousness that any individual can be saved. In fact, no person has ever been saved except by faith in Christ, including Abraham and all those who lived before him. Though they did not understand the Gospel as we do, they believed God on the basis of what He had revealed to them.

Thus Paul wrote, "The Scripture foresaw that God would justify the Gentiles by faith, and announced the Gospel in advance to Abraham" (Gal. 3:8). And since Christ has now come, we can live in the full light and freedom of that reality.

If you are relying on works for your salvation, acknowledge that you cannot save yourself. Trust Christ to save you. Believe that He died for your sins and rose again that you might have eternal life. This prayer will help you:

Dear God,

I acknowledge that *nothing* I can do in and of myself can save me from my sins. I thank You for sending Your perfect Son Jesus Christ to die for my sins. I thank You that He is alive today and I now put my faith in Him and what He has done for me. Thank You for making me righteous in Your sight.

Signed _____ Date _____

There's a second area to think about in terms of personal application of these truths. Perhaps you have trusted Christ for salvation—now or sometime in the past—but now you are trying to keep yourself saved by adhering to the Law. That is impossible; Christians cannot live perfect lives. You are not only saved by faith in Christ's finished work on the Cross, but are *kept saved* by that finished work. Eternal life for the Christian begins the moment he believes and will always be *eternal*.

Christians are to do good works, and *can do* good works, but with a whole new source of motivation and inner strength. When a person becomes a Christian, "The grace of God that brings salvation . . . teaches him to say 'No' to ungodliness and worldly passions, and to live self-controlled, upright, and godly lives in this present age" (Titus 2:11-12).

What is the new source of motivation and inner strength to help you do good works? The same grace that saved you! When you understand that grace, you can never be the same again. "Therefore," Paul wrote, "I urge you, brothers, *in view of God's mercy,* to offer yourselves as living sacrifices, holy and pleasing to God. . . . Do not conform any longer to the pattern of this world, but be transformed by the renewing of your mind" (Rom. 12:1-2).

Are you allowing God's grace and love to motivate you to live this kind of life? If you are, you are not only saved by grace through faith, but you are also allowing God to work in you "to will and to act according to His good purpose" (Phil. 2:13). And part of God's plan is that you "love one another" just as Christ loved you in order that "all men will know" that you are Christ's disciple.

As I have loved you, so you must love one another.
John 13:34b

2

Christ's Example of Love

Following Christ's new commandment to His men to love one another, He made another statement—which at that moment in their lives was probably very threatening. "As I have loved you," said Jesus, "so you must love one another" (John 13:34).

What was Jesus saying? More important, what did the disciples *hear* Him saying? Why would this injunction be threatening? From our perspective on biblical history, we can analyze His statement much more thoroughly—and objectively—than those who heard it the very first time.

For example, we have Paul's Letter to the Ephesians which gives us an extensive commentary on how to love as Christ loved. He exhorted these Christians to "live a life of love, just as Christ loved us and gave Himself up for us as a fragrant offering and sacrifice to God" (Eph. 5:2). Later he told husbands to love their wives "just as Christ loved the church and gave Himself up for her" (5:25).

The Apostle John never forgot Christ's words in the Upper Room. Though he did not understand their full meaning then, he did later. Again and again, in his first epistle, he told Christians to "love one another." And his statement and definition of Christ's words at the Last Supper show that he really understood what Christ meant. "This is how we know what love is: Jesus

Christ laid down His life for us. And we ought to lay down our lives for our brothers'' (1 John 3:16).

But what did John and the other disciples understand about Christ's statement in the Upper Room when they first heard it? Their comprehension was limited and restricted to what had happened in their relationship with Christ to that moment in their lives. The "old commandment"? This they understood! They were Jews. They had "been entrusted with the very words of God" (Rom. 3:2). They understood the "Law and the prophets''—at least from the standpoint of content.

However, it would take time and experience for them to understand the ultimate purpose of the old commandment, and the relationship between the Law of Moses and the truth revealed in Jesus Christ.

When Christ made these statements, they didn't understand His coming death or why He had to die. Consequently, they couldn't understand fully the "new commandment" Jesus was talking about. Actually, they knew very little of what Jesus really meant—either in the area of content or experience. But they were soon to learn.

The Setting for Christ's Love (John 13:1-3)

It was time for the Passover feast. This was an important event in Israel's history that commemorated their deliverance from slavery in Egypt and particularly their escape from God's judgment when He slew all the firstborn. Jesus was about to use this memorial event to teach His disciples some important truths about His own life—what was about to happen to Him and why He had come into this world. The Passover pictured God's ultimate redemptive plan. Christ's shed blood would protect all who appropriate its power from God's judgment.

Christ had already demonstrated His love for them. Choosing them, teaching them, protecting them, and meeting their needs were all reflections of His love. Just the fact that He had "made Himself nothing . . . being made in human likeness" and walked and talked with these men, was one of His greatest acts of love yet known in the universe (Phil. 2:7). Jesus Christ was "in very nature God" and yet "did not consider equality with God something to be grasped" (2:6). The fact that He came to earth in human form and walked among men was an act of love.

But at that moment in their lives the disciples did not understand even this. They did not really comprehend Christ's love. If they had, they would not have argued with one another "as to which of them was considered to be greatest" (Luke 22:24).

Think of it. Jesus Christ was about to die for the sins of the world, and His disciples—at that very moment at the Passover feast—were vying for His attention and trying to put one another down.

Jesus Christ knew all about their weaknesses, their selfish motives, and their lack of love for one another, and He loved them just the same. His very tolerance regarding their weaknesses was an act of love. But now He was about to demonstrate His love in a way that they *could* understand—and never forget.

Earlier Christ had sent Peter and John into Jerusalem to prepare for the Passover meal. No doubt this act in itself had created some feelings of pride in these two men and some jealousy in the hearts of the other disciples. They had found a room, "a large upper room, all furnished," just as Christ has said they would (22:7-12).

In that sense they had nothing to be proud of. They were human instruments being used by God. Like all humans, they wanted to take credit for what God had done.

This was the setting in which Jesus Christ in picture form "showed them the full extent of His love" (John 13:1). They could not yet grasp the full meaning of the Cross. Neither could they comprehend the significance of the broken bread and the wine. But they could not miss Christ's example of love.

The Demonstration of Christ's Love (John 13:4-11)
Sometime during the meal, Christ got up from the table and "began to wash His disciples' feet, drying them with a towel that

was wrapped around Him" (John 13:5). This was no minor incident. You see, this was ordinarily a job for a slave. In an oriental household, guests were customarily welcomed in this way. Since they walked through the dusty streets in footwear that would hardly compare with our modern shoes, their feet were usually very dirty. Remember that the streets were not only used by people but by animals of all sorts and sizes. Consequently, guests who entered a home had their feet washed by one of the household servants.

Since this was a private meal in a borrowed facility, there was no household servant. No doubt Christ had waited for one of the disciples to volunteer to carry out this role. The basin was there. So was the towel. But there was one major problem—the absence of a servant.

This was Christ's opportunity. He became that Servant. He washed their feet, including Judas's. Though Christ encountered initial resistance from Peter, He received immediate cooperation when He said, "Unless I wash you, you have no part with Me" (13:8). Though Peter responded with his usual impetuousness, he was yet to learn the full meaning of what Christ had done.

Later, they would fully understand their "attitude should be the same as that of Christ Jesus, who . . . made Himself nothing, taking the very nature of a servant" (Phil. 2:5-7).

The Meaning of Christ's Love (John 13:12-17)
In this act of servanthood Christ demonstrated His ultimate purpose in coming to this world. John began his account with these words: "Having loved His own who were in the world, He now showed them the full extent of His love" (John 13:1). Inherent in this experience was a picture of the Cross—Christ's willingness to die for those He loved. Paul interpreted this for us when he wrote, "And being found in appearance as a man, He humbled Himself and became obedient to death—even death on a cross" (Phil. 2:8).

But this is more than a picture of Christ's love for us. It is a lesson in *how* to love as Christ loved. It was against this backdrop that Christ said a few minutes later, "A new commandment I give you: love one another. As I have loved you, so you must love one another" (John 13:34).

The practical outworking of this statement begins with the nitty-gritty of life. For the disciples, it involved a willingness to wash one another's feet. "I have set you an example," Jesus concluded, "that you should do as I have done for you" (13:15).

In many respects this was a shocking experience for the disciples. It threatened them, especially in view of their prideful argument. It violated their cultural tradition. It hit at the very heart of their self-centeredness, their desire to dominate and control one another. As Dr. Merrill Tenney comments, "They were ready to fight for a throne, but not for a towel!" (*John: The Gospel of Belief*. Eerdmans, 1953, p. 199)

But this is what Christianity is all about. It crosses all cultural and social lines. This is why slaves and masters sat side by side in the New Testament church (Eph. 6:9). They were now brothers in Christ. For the same reason, poor people occupied the front seats of the church along with the rich (James 2:1-4). Wives sat beside their husbands with pride and dignity. And Jews and Gentiles were no longer enemies. "There is neither Jew nor Greek, slave nor free, male nor female, for you are all one in Christ Jesus" (Gal. 3:28).

Loving as Christ Loved

What does it mean today to "love as Christ loved"? Obviously, few people are called on to pay the ultimate sacrifice for others—the sacrifice of death—though this certainly has happened over the years.

On the evening of April 15, 1912, during its first trip from England to New York City, what was called an unsinkable scagoing vessel struck an iceberg and began to go down. That ship was the *Titanic*. The tragedy happened about 1,600 miles northeast of New York City in the heart of the Atlantic Ocean. The iceberg tore a 300-foot gash in the ship's hull. Unfortunately, there were lifeboats for less than half of the 2,200 passengers. Two-and-one-half hours after the impact, 1,490 people went to a watery grave. Most that survived were women and children.

That horrible night there were men who scrambled and sought to save themselves, caring nothing of others. But there were also those who willingly stepped aside to let others be saved, knowing they would die. Fathers kissed their wives and children good-bye. Friends embraced for the last time and separated, knowing they would not see each other again on this earth. Many willingly paid the ultimate sacrifice for their friends—death.

Note Christ's words to His disciples a little while later after they had left the Upper Room. He reinforced the lesson He had just taught them. "My command is this: Love each other as I have loved you. Greater love has no one than this, that One lay down His life for His friends" (John 15:12-13).

Probably few of us will be called upon to actually die for others—though this is certainly not beyond the realm of possibility. Many Christians before us have faced this kind of persecution.

But what about now? What are we doing to "love as Christ loved" in the daily routine of life? Peter was quick to respond to Christ's challenge by saying, "Lord . . . I will lay down my life for You" (13:37). But a few minutes earlier he had not even been willing to initiate the process of washing Jesus' feet. Peter knew there was a need. He knew the custom, and no doubt he saw the wash basin and the towel. But he was not willing, nor were the others. This is why Christ's statement must have been both startling and humbling.

Later Peter demonstrated that his attempts at love were very superficial. His words sounded good, but if he had meant what he said, he would not have denied Christ three times.

Words are cheap and easy to utter. It's relatively easy to say "I love you" and "I will do anything for you" when personal sacrifice is yet future. And it's probably easier to be a servant (even unto death) when we have no choice. But what about the ordinary stuff out of which our human relationships are made?

A Personal Response

Family relationships. Think for a moment about your relationships. They really begin in the family. What are you willing to do for those you *say* you love? And remember, Christ loved His disciples unconditionally, even when they were inconsistent, selfish, proud, impatient with one another, unkind, envious, rude, and untrusting.

Check yourself. In what ways are you loving as Christ loved? In what ways are you being selfish, just like the disciples were in their relationships?

_____ I want to be served rather than to serve.

_____ I want to be first rather than last.

_____ I want more than others, rather than less.

_____ I want to be honored rather than looking for opportunities to honor others.

_____ I want to be the center of attention rather than giving others attention.

_____ I want what I want *now*, rather than making sure others' needs are met first.

Relationships with other Christians. What about other Christians? You may often *say* you love others. What about your life-style? "Dear children," wrote the Apostle John, "let us not love with words or tongue but with actions and in truth" (1 John 3:18).

_____ I am willing to serve others in love even when I am not given public recognition.

_____ I'm actually looking for opportunities to be a servant.

_____ I am praying for other Christians, at least as much as I pray for myself.

_____ I am willing to become involved in other Christians' lives.

_____ I am sharing a significant percentage of my money so that the body of Christ can function adequately.

_____ I am using my other material possessions to minster to others; in other words, I am practicing hospitality.

Relationships with non-Christians. What about your relationships with non-Christians? The Bible says you are to "do good to all people" (Gal. 6:10). Paul went on to say that you should especially do good to the "family of believers." But the fact remains that you are also to love non-Christians. Christ, of course, set the supreme example. He not only died for His friends but also for His enemies.

_____ I have asked God to help me "love my neighbor as myself."

_____ I'm actually reaching out to establish friendships with non-Christians.

_____ I am concerned that non-Christians understand the Gospel and become Christians.

_____ I make an effort to meet new people—both Christians and non-Christians.

Action Step. Once again think about John's definition of love in his first epistle: "This is how we know what love is: Jesus Christ laid down His life for us. And we ought to lay down our lives for our brothers" (1 John 3:16).

As you review the checklists, think about one thing you can do immediately to "lay down your life" for someone else. Make this your "foot washing" experience. Before you can serve others in the bigger areas of life, you need to begin where the disciples began—by serving others in the nitty-gritty relationships of life. Write out one step you are going to take to begin to "love others as Christ loved you."

_____

_____

_____

_____

_____

_____

_____

All men will know that you are My disciples if you love one another.

John 13:35

3

Reflecting Christ's Love

Jesus Christ had an ultimate purpose in mind when he gave His disciples a new commandment, telling them to love one another as He had loved them. That purpose was to reveal to all mankind who He really was—and is. Though He had walked among people, demonstrating His love for them and telling them of His reasons for coming into the world—to save them from their sins—He would soon no longer be visible. He was going "to leave this world and go to the Father" (John 13:1).

How then would people know of Christ's love for them? How could He "speak" though absent? Christ *did* have a plan—a beautiful plan. "All men will know that you are My disciples," He said, "if you love one another" (13:35).

Demonstrating His Love

The most important word in this statement is the word *My*. The Lord was referring to Himself. He did not say, "All men will know that you are disciples." Rather, He said, "All men will know that you are *My* disciples." You see, there have been *many* disciples over the years, since the word simply means a "learner." A disciple was a student of some teacher. For example, Socrates was called a disciple of Homer.

In the religious world of Jesus' day there were disciples of the

Pharisees, and disciples of John the Baptist (Luke 5:33). The Pharisees themselves claimed to be "disciples of Moses" (John 9:28).

But there was no other teacher like Jesus Christ. The 12 men who were *His* disciples were not ordinary learners. Yes, they were ordinary in the sense of being human beings like you and me. In fact, several of them were simple fishermen. They were not part of the intelligentsia of their day. But they were *extraordinary* men in the sense that they had been taught by the One "who became flesh" and lived among them.

Later, when Christ had returned to the Father, the Apostle John understood this reality. "We have seen His glory, the glory of the one and only Son, who came from the Father, full of grace and truth" (1:14). Furthermore, when the Pharisees observed the behavior of these men after Christ's return to heaven, they sensed "that they were unschooled, ordinary men." But they also "were astonished and they took note that these men had been with Jesus" (Acts 4:13). These men were indeed disciples of Jesus Christ.

Christ's unique plan was that non-Christians come to know of His love through Christians in proper relationship with one another. Though Christ would no longer be physically present, people could learn of His love through His followers who would continue to love one another as He had loved them while He was on the earth.

This is why John wrote, "Dear friends, since God so loved us, we also ought to love one another. No one has ever seen God; but if we love each other, God lives in us and His love is made complete in us" (1 John 4:11-12).

The implication in John's statement is obvious. Non-Christians can "see" the invisible God, through Christians who make Him visible because of His presence in their hearts and lives. This is why Christ was concerned that His disciples love one another as He had loved them. In this way, all men would know they were *His* disciples—not just any teacher's disciples.

You see, Christ demonstrated and taught a way of life that

distinguished Him from all other teachers of His day. That distinction was love. With the exception of John the Baptist, who said that Christ "must become greater" and he "must become less" important (John 3:30), all other teachers of Jesus' day were basically "self" oriented.

Christ was "others" oriented. He "did not come to be served, but to serve, and to give His life as a ransom for many" (Matt. 20:28). This He demonstrated throughout His earthly life, though there were many people who did not recognize this fact (including His own men) until He died and rose again. He was indeed a unique Teacher, one who willingly gave His life, not only for His friends, but for His enemies (John 15:13). Consequently, if His disciples would love one another as He had loved them, then it would be obvious whose disciples they really were.

Relating to One Another

The fact that Jesus Christ chose 12 men to initially represent Him on earth leads to another important observation. If He had only developed one disciple, He would never have been able to say, "Love one another." An individual Christian is limited in the way he reflects Christ to others. We need the fellowship of other Christians to experience the quality of love Christ wants us to know.

It is true that individual Christians *can* love non-Christians by reflecting Christ's love (Rom. 5:8). But that kind of love is limited, due to the very nature of the relationship that *must* exist between Christians and non-Christians. We have nothing in common at the deeper levels of life. In fact, we are to be separate from the world. We are not to "love the world or anything in the world. If anyone loves the world, the love of the Father is not in him"(1 John 2:15).

Paul emphasized this same point when he wrote to the Corinthians. "Do not be yoked together with unbelievers. For what do righteousness and wickedness have in common? Or what fellowship can light have with darkness? What harmony is there between Christ and Belial? What does a believer have in common with an unbeliever?" (2 Cor. 6:14-15)

Consequently, our love for the person outside of Christ can only function at a superficial level. We can and should "do good" to non-Christians (Gal. 6:10)—feeding them when they're hungry, caring for them when they're sick, advising them when they're in trouble. Furthermore, we are not to retaliate with vengeance when we are mistreated by non-Christians. This is what Christ meant when He told us to love our enemies and to do good to those who hate us (Luke 6:27).

How then can we communicate Christ's *deep* and *abiding love* to the unbeliever? As we've seen from Scripture, we can never love a non-Christian as Christ loved us. Only God's Son could do that. Nor can we love non-Christians in the same way as we love other believers.

But by loving one another in the presence of non-Christians we can communicate God's love to them. There are no fellowship restrictions on this kind of love, except of course, moral restrictions. We can have deep and abiding fellowship with one another because "our fellowship is with the Father and with His Son, Jesus Christ" (1 John 1:3).

The church—strictly defined—was not launched until the Day of Pentecost. But the ability of believers to function in proper relationship with one another began earlier. In the same way, the concept of the *body* of Christ was unknown to Christ's disciples before the Holy Spirit came. But the groundwork was laid in their lives before Christ went to the cross.

When the Holy Spirit came following Christ's ascension, then the full outworking of Christ's teaching in John 13 became a dynamic reality. What Christ said to the disciples in the Upper Room was to be the normal way of life among the larger group of disciples who were eventually called Christians (Acts 11:26). This word in itself distinguished *Christ's disciples* from all other disciples.

Significantly, it seems Christ's disciples were first identified as Christians by nonbelievers. The word refers to "followers of

Christ." It is formed directly from the word *Christ* and the *ianos* ending, which is from the Greek and is used only with proper names. For example, the followers (or disciples) of Herod were called "Herodians" (Mark 3:6). The important observation, of course, is that non-Christians indeed recognized the followers of Christ as *His* disciples. The name they gave believers verifies that they were reflecting Christ.

Reflecting Christ's Love Today

Jesus Christ launched the Christian movement with 12 people who were to love one another, demonstrating His love to *"all* men." In this way, believers could reach those who hadn't heard of Christ. Also, they could exemplify God's love to those followers who were still uncommitted.

Christ had many followers, but some were not committed to Him. In fact, on one occasion when Jesus was teaching some profound truths regarding Himself, "Many of His disciples said, 'This is a hard teaching. Who can accept it?' " And later we read that "from this time many of His disciples turned back and no longer followed Him" (John 6:60, 66).

Just so, many people who claim to be Christians no longer follow Christ. To them, many of Christ's teachings are too difficult to accept. They find it hard to obey Him. They have not yet learned to love Jesus Christ as they should, nor have they learned to love other Christians at the deeper levels of life.

Just as those uncommitted followers in Jesus' day needed a corporate model, many "Christians" today also need a corporate model. God's plan was that the Twelve serve as that model to others. Today God wants those who are closest to Him to be models to others.

The most direct application of this truth focuses on the leadership of the church. God's design is that each local body of believers be led by mature people who love one another and who in turn reflect that love to others. The apostles laid the foundation for the church "at large" (Eph. 2:20).

But later, men called elders or overseers were to shepherd local churches and model Christ's teachings before others. This is why multiple leadership in the church is so vital and important. One spiritual leader cannot model love as Christ intended, any more than one disciple could have modeled that love.

But Christ's injunction applies to *all* Christians. We are all important in Christ's body, and as a "total body" we are to reflect Christ's love. That small band of disciples who met with Jesus in the Upper Room soon swelled to 120 following Christ's death and resurrection. They too were in an upper room, planning and seeking God's will when the Holy Spirit first came upon them (Acts 2:1-4).

God wants His spiritual body to grow, both in numbers and in maturity. And when it does, its influence will be felt and sensed first by Christians who are yet on the periphery and second by those who have never decided to follow Christ.

People who truly care for one another attract attention. In fact, Satan does his best to simulate these conditions among people who are involved in false religions. Let me illustrate. I once heard of a young man who graduated from a well-known Bible school and planned to go to South America as a missionary. However, before he left, he spent some time visiting a Mormon community to observe their methods. He was so impressed with their care and concern and "love" for one another that he gave up his relationships in the evangelical community and became a Mormon.

How could this be? Wherever the principle of love is practiced, even among non-Christians, it attracts others. Satan has done his best throughout history to cause non-Christians to simulate "Christ's love" so people would become involved in false religions—in this case, a religion that denies that Jesus Christ is God in the flesh and one with the Father.

A Personal Response
Where are you presently in this ever-growing experience? How committed are you to Jesus Christ and to members of His body? If you claim to be a Christian and yet are not concerned about

other Christians—their needs and their hurts, their joys and their sorrows—then you are really not loving other Christians as you should. You are not obeying Christ. And if you do not obey, you do not love (John 15:10). "For anyone who does not love his brother, whom he has seen, cannot love God, whom he has not seen" (1 John 4:20).

What evidence is there in your life that you are loving other Christians as you should (outside of your immediate family)? List five things you have done in the last two weeks that reflect this love:

1. _____

2 _____

3. _____

4. _____

5. _____

This is to My Father's glory, that you bear much fruit, showing yourselves to be My disciples.

John 15:8

4

Bearing Much Fruit

In the Upper Room with the 12 disciples, Jesus presented a divine plan for making Himself known to all people. Then He told the disciples that He was going away "to prepare a place" for them (John 14:1-4). He clarified His relationship to God the Father (14:9). And He promised them He would send the Holy Spirit who would continue to teach them and guide them. He "will teach you all things" said Jesus, "and will remind you of everything I have said to you" (14:26).

The Illustration and Command

Eventually, they left the Upper Room (14:31) and made their way to the outskirts of the city. While they were walking along, Jesus again underscored the fact that He wanted them to make Him known to others. "This is to My Father's glory, that you bear much fruit, showing yourselves to be My disciples" (15:8). On the surface it may appear that this is what He had just said in the Upper Room. In a sense it was, but the Lord was adding a new dimension to His previous statement.

During the Passover meal, Jesus had used the foot-washing incident to help the disciples understand the meaning of His love and how they should demonstrate that love to one another. This time Jesus used the story of the vine and the branches.

Imagine what may have happened. As they walked along discussing what Christ had just taught them, they passed a vineyard that had been freshly pruned. It may have been a clear moonlit night. The gardener had been hard at work that day, cutting away dead branches and pruning those that had been alive with fruit. Perhaps some ashes still glimmered and smoldered where the gardener had burned the dead brush.

As frequently happened in His teaching ministry, Christ used a natural opportunity to make a spiritual point. The actual circumstances were so vivid in the disciples' minds that He seemingly didn't have to set the stage verbally. He simply applied the truth directly: "I am the true Vine," He said, "My Father is the Gardener. He cuts off every branch in Me that bears no fruit, while every branch that does bear fruit He trims clean so that it will be even more fruitful" (15:1-2).

Back on the farm in Indiana where I grew up, we had an orchard. Running the full length of the orchard was a grape arbor. But no one ever took care of the orchard or the arbor. In fact, when I was a kid I sat in the plum trees and ate grapes. The reason I could engage in this rather strange behavior was that the grapevines were never pruned. They grew wild and eventually there were more grapevines in the plum trees than plum branches. You can imagine what happened to both the grape arbor and the fruit trees. Both were restricted in their production of good fruit. True, they did prosper, but it wasn't quality fruit, nor was there quantity.

Jesus' concern was that His disciples bear much fruit. He used this natural illustration to get His point across.

Judas, though he had appeared to be a "fruit-bearing branch," had already left the group and was making final plans to betray Christ. His tragic destiny lay just ahead.

But the 11 who remained belonged to Christ. Though they were limited in their understanding of God's redemptive plan in Christ, they were represented in the allegory as those branches that had been freshly pruned. "You are already clean," Jesus said, "because of the word I have spoken to you" (15:3). There was no doubt about their relationship to Christ. They were *His* disciples. Neither was there any doubt regarding Christ's plan for them. They were to bear fruit—*much fruit*—demonstrating to others they were indeed intimately related to Him. Though He would be absent from this world, He would be visibly present in and through their lives.

In this illustration Christ made it very clear that the Gardener is His Father (15:1). He also made it very clear that He is the true Vine. And it is obvious that the freshly pruned branches represent the 11 disciples who had not forsaken Him (15:2-3). But Christ did not define the word *fruit* as He did the other aspects and elements in this allegory. What did Christ actually mean?

To answer this question from Scripture we need to look at the immediate context—at what Christ had already said about His plan for demonstrating to others that He was indeed the Christ and that these men were *His* disciples. Notice the similarity in these two statements:

"All men will know that you are My disciples if you love one another" (John 13:25).

"This is to My Father's glory, that you bear much fruit, showing yourselves to be My disciples" (John 15:8).

Since both of these statements were made by Christ to His disciples within a relatively short period of time, it is logical to conclude that the fruit referred to their love for one another. Furthermore, this is verified by Christ's statements immediately following His illustration of the vineyard:

"As the Father has loved Me, so have I loved you. Now *remain in My love*. If you obey My commands, you will *remain in My love*, just as I have obeyed My Father's commands and remain in His love . . . My command is this: *Love each other* as I have loved you. Greater love has no one than this that One lay down His life for His friends . . . You did not choose Me, but I chose you to go and bear fruit—fruit that will last . . . This is My command: *Love each other*" (15:9-17).

A Deeper Dimension of Love

Frequently, when we read in Scripture that we are to love one another, we think primarily of ways in which we can demonstrate kindness to a brother or sister in Christ. In fact, this is the essence of the "one another" concepts in the New Testament. We are to "be devoted to one another in brotherly love" and "honor one another" above ourselves (Rom. 12:10); we are to "accept one another" just as Christ accepted us (15:7); we are to "greet one another" (16:16); we are to "serve one another" (Gal. 5:13) and to "carry each other's burdens" (6:2); we are to "be patient" (Eph. 4:2) and "submit to one another" (5:21); we are to "encourage one another"(1 Thes. 4:18; 5:11) and to "show hospitality to one another" (1 Peter 4:9).

All of these injunctions, when practiced by believers toward one another, certainly reflect the kind of love Christ was talking about in the Upper Room. However, these concepts represent only one dimension of Christ's love. There is yet another in Scripture—the dimension of righteousness, holiness, and purity in our relationships with one another. I feel that Christ certainly had this dimension of love in mind when He said, "This is to My Father's glory, that you bear much fruit, showing yourselves to be My disciples" (John 15:8).

Paul developed this dimension of love in his letter to the Philippian Christians, particularly in his prayer for them. "And this is my prayer: that your love may abound more and more in knowledge and depth of insight, so that you may be able to discern what is best and may be pure and blameless until the Day of Christ, filled with the fruit of righteousness that comes through Jesus Christ—to the glory and praise of God" (Phil. 1:9-11). Let's compare Jesus' words with Paul's prayer.

First, Jesus' desire for His disciples was that they bear fruit, *more* fruit, and *much* fruit. In the same way, Paul prayed that the Philippians' love would abound *more and more*.

Second, Jesus wanted His disciples to "bear much *fruit*." Paul prayed that the Philippians would be filled with the *fruit* of righteousness.

Third, Jesus said this kind of fruit-bearing would be to His "Father's *glory*." Paul wrote that the "fruit of righteousness" would be to the "*glory* and praise of God."

There is, then, a dimension of love in our corporate and spiritual growth that goes beyond devotion, honor, kindness, acceptance, serving, burden-bearing, tolerance, forgiveness, submission, encouragement, and hospitality. It is the dimension of righteousness in our relationships with one another—involving honesty, integrity, and purity.

Paul included that dimension when he referred to the "fruit of the Spirit" in his letter to the Galatians. Non-Christians may say they "love one another," but it is often characterized by acts of the sinful nature—"sexual immorality, impurity and debauchery," and "drunkenness, orgies, and the like" (Gal. 5:19-21). But, wrote Paul, the fruit of the Spirit in Christian relationships involves not only love, joy, peace, patience, kindness, and gentleness, but also goodness and self-control (5:22). And then to underscore what he really meant, Paul wrote, "Those who belong to Christ Jesus have crucified the sinful nature with its passions and desires" (5:24).

There's another unique correlation between Paul's prayer for the Philippians and his desire for the Roman Christians. For the Philippians, his prayer was that their knowledge and insight would enable them to "discern what is best" in the area of Christian relationships. The word *discern* in this prayer is the same basic word used in Romans 12:1-2. Here Paul urged the Roman Christians to offer themselves as "living sacrifices, holy and pleasing to God" and not to "conform any longer to the pattern of this world, but be transformed" by the renewing of their minds. "Then," Paul stated, "you will be able to test and approve what God's will is—His good, pleasing, and perfect will."

It seems obvious from other scriptural statements that the *fruit* Jesus referred to involved a dimension of love which included righteousness and holiness. This interpretation also parallels closely Paul's use of the word *fruit*, when he wrote, "Live as children of light (for the *fruit* of the light consists in all goodness, righteousness, and truth)." And to draw a contrast, he wrote— "Have nothing to do with the *fruitless* deeds of darkness, but rather expose them" (Eph. 5:8-11).

So far, we have seen clearly that Jesus Christ was laying a foundation for effective evangelism and Christian witness. This foundation involves a "corporate visibility"—Christians in proper relationship with one another. Christian love among believers can and should be deep, intimate, and meaningful. But what makes it truly Christlike love is that it is pure, righteous, and holy. It must never exploit or use others for selfish ends.

A Basis for Answered Prayer

Having right attitudes and actions among Christians is frequently stated in Scripture as a condition for answered prayer. This was true in Old Testament days as well. The psalmist acknowledged this truth when he said, "If I regard wickedness in my heart, the Lord will not hear" (Ps. 66:18). In the New Testament Peter exhorted Christian husbands to love their wives and treat them "with respect." Why? "So," he wrote, "that nothing will hinder your prayers" (1 Peter 3:7).

Twice in Christ's discourse regarding the vine and the branches, He also made reference to answered prayer. In fact, being a "fruit-bearing" Christian was stated as a condition for answered prayer. Jesus said, "If you remain in Me and My words remain in you, ask whatever you wish, and it will be given you" (John 15:7-8). And at the conclusion of this discourse He said, "I chose you to go and bear fruit—fruit that will last. Then the Father will give you whatever you ask in My name" (15:16).

One proof for non-Christians that Christ is truly God's Son and our Saviour is the fact of answered prayer. There's no greater apologetic before the watching world than Christians who "love one another deeply" (1 Peter 1:22; 4:8), and who, in Christian community, pray for one another and see answers to their prayers. This not only makes a dynamic impact on non-Christians, but also strengthens and encourages other Christians.

Like Mary we can say, "For the mighty One has done great things for me—holy is His name" (Luke 1:49).

Bearing Fruit Today

What does Christ's illustration regarding the vine and the branches say to us? It is true that the most direct application is that, as modern Christians, we too must "bear much fruit, showing ourselves to be Christ's disciples"—the fruit of righteousness, reflecting God's holiness. When people see us relating properly with one another, they should be able to see Christ's righteousness.

Let's focus for a moment on answered prayer. The Lord made certain promises to the 11 apostles that do not apply totally to our lives today. The apostles, along with certain other New Testament believers, received special power to do miracles and other signs among unbelievers. In some cases, the "prayer promises" Jesus made to these believers were related to their special calling as apostles and their special power to perform miracles.

But answers to prayer were received by other believers throughout the New Testament churches. Though we do not and cannot understand completely the concept of prayer, we know God honors and answers according to His will.

I believe that the love Christ talked about in John 13 and 15, both in the family setting as well as in the local church, is a condition God sets for answered prayer. I cannot explain it fully, because I cannot fully understand God. But I know by experience that God honors this principle.

I also know by experience that answered prayer powerfully demonstrates to non-Christians that Jesus Christ is who He said He is. People are attracted to what works. They are very pragmatic in their religious quests.

I remember visiting a Christian Science church to observe their service. They have regular "sharing" services where people express publicly what Christian Science is doing for them. This attracts people to their religion. How much more so should the functioning body of Christ attract people to the One who said, "I am the Way and the Truth and the Life" (John 14:6). And answered prayer is one valid proof that cannot be ignored.

A Personal Response

Following is a checklist that reflects the fruit (John 15) which enables others to know that you are indeed Christ's disciple. With each quality is Christ's "progressive" criterion for measuring your personal lifestyle as well as your corporate and "body" witness in the world. Obviously, to increase our "body visibility" each one of us must begin with his own life personally. Check yourself. To what extent are you contributing to the corporate fruitfulness of the whole body?

	I AM BEARING FRUIT	I AM MORE "FRUITFUL" TODAY THAN I WAS SIX MONTHS AGO	I FEEL I AM BEARING MUCH FRUIT	I CANNOT ANSWER

GALATIANS 5:22-23

But the fruit of the spirit is . . .

LOVE
JOY
PEACE
PATIENCE
KINDNESS
GOODNESS
FAITHFULNESS
GENTLENESS
SELF-CONTROL

EPHESIANS 5:9

For the fruit of the light consists in all . . .

GOODNESS
RIGHTEOUSNESS
TRUTH

PHILIPPIANS 1:9-11

My goal is to be "filled with the fruit of right-eousness that comes through Jesus Christ," reflected by:

MORE AND MORE KNOWLEDGE
OF HIS WILL
DEPTH OF INSIGHT
DISCERNING WHAT IS BEST
PURITY
BLAMELESSNESS (A GOOD REPUTATION)

May they be brought to complete unity to let the world know that You sent Me and have loved them even as You have loved Me.

John 17:23

5

Letting the World Know

Christ's concern both for His disciples and their mission was beautifully expressed in His high priestly prayer in John 17. He first stated this concern in the Upper Room when He told them to love one another. Then He illustrated this concern as they left the Upper Room and walked through Jerusalem to the outskirts of the city, no doubt passing a grape arbor. "This is to My Father's glory," He said, pointing to the freshly pruned vines, "that you bear much fruit, showing yourselves to be My disciples" (John 15:8).

His culminating statement about their witness in the world was made in His prayer to the Father. "May they be brought to complete unity to let the world know that You sent Me and have loved them even as You have loved Me" (17:23).

Jesus' Prayer for the Disciples

Jesus prayed first for the 11 men His Father gave Him "out of the world" (17:6). At last they had believed in their hearts that He had come from God, that He was indeed Deity (16:30-31). Thus Jesus could pray, "Now they know that everything You have given Me comes from You. For I gave them the words You gave Me and they accepted them. They knew with certainty that I came from You, and they believed that You sent Me" (17:7-8).

47

It had been a three-and-one-half year process. Many times the disciples had told Jesus they believed in Him, but the Lord, knowing their hearts, perceived they did not understand who He really was. Now they did. They understood clearly He was one with the Father. Consequently, Jesus now prayed, "Holy Father, protect them by the power of Your name—the name You gave Me—so that they may be one as We are One" (17:11).

Jesus did not pray that His Father would take them out of the world, but rather that He would protect them as they remained behind to carry out His purpose (17:15). "As You sent Me into the world," Jesus prayed, "I have sent them into the world" (17:18). Earlier in His prayer, Christ had stated His purpose for coming into this world. "Now this is eternal life: that they may know You, the only true God, and Jesus Christ, whom You have sent" (17:3).

Jesus' Prayer for All Believers

John 17 records one of those unique occasions when Christ spoke directly about Christians living today. Many times His statements were directed at those who were with Him, though most of what He said applies to all Christians.

But in His high priestly prayer there was no question whom He had in mind. "My prayer is not for them [the 11 disciples] alone. I pray for those also [Christians of all time] who will believe in Me through their message" (17:20). With these words Jesus was praying for us—and for every person who has ever believed either by hearing those 11 men speak, or by reading the Scriptures which several of them wrote.

What was this "message" Christ referred to in John 17:20? In essence it was what the disciples had just come to believe—that Christ was one with the Father and that He had come from the Father. At this point Christ prayed the same prayer for all believers (present and future) that He had just prayed for the 11, "That all of them may be one, Father, just as You are in Me and I am in You" (17:21a).

But even more significant than His prayer that we "be one"

was the reason He prayed for this unity—*"that the world may believe"* that the Father had sent Him (17:21b). And to make sure this purpose was clear in the minds and hearts of all of us who have believed in Christ, Jesus prayed, "May they be brought to complete unity *to let the world* know that You sent Me and have loved them even as You have loved Me" (17:23).

There is no clearer evangelistic statement in the whole New Testament. Christ's desire was that those, who had not yet believed in Him, would come to faith by means of the love and unity demonstrated by Christians—beginning with His 11 men and all those who later would become believers.

Jesus' Claim to be God

To understand Christ's prayer in John 17, we must understand His relationship to God. It is no secret who He claimed to be. To Nicodemus, He had said that He was God's "only Son" and that whoever believed in Him would have eternal life (John 3:16). To the Samaritan woman, He affirmed that He was indeed the promised Messiah (the Christ). If she believed in Him, He would give her water to drink that would become "a spring of water welling up to eternal life" (4:14).

To the multitude He had miraculously fed with the bread and the fish, He declared: "I am the Bread of Life. He who comes to Me will never go hungry, and he who believes in Me will never be thirsty" (6:35). On another occasion, He spoke to the crowd that gathered to hear Him and said, "I am the Light of the World. Whoever follows Me will never walk in darkness but will have the light of life" (8:12).

Christ's most startling statements about Himself were yet to come. As He spoke to the Jewish leaders of His day, He left no questions in their minds regarding His claims. "Before Abraham was born, I AM!" He said to an angry group of critics (8:58). With this claim, He identified Himself as the God who had told Moses at the burning bush to say to the Israelites that "I AM has sent me to you" (Ex. 3:14).

Later, Christ made His message to the Jews even clearer. "If you are the Christ, tell us plainly," they demanded (John 10:24). Christ responded with His most direct statement to date. "I and the Father are one" (10:30).

But Christ did not rely on words alone to convince people that He was the Son of God and the Saviour of the world. He demonstrated His deity and verified His words with miraculous signs.

John recorded seven miracles that were uniquely designed to cause people to believe that Christ was God in the flesh. First, Christ changed water to wine at a wedding in Cana (2:1-11). Then, John recorded that He healed a royal official's son while the boy was in one town and Jesus was in another (4:43-54). Next, He caused a man to walk who had been crippled for 38 years (5:1-14). Then He fed over 5,000 people with "five small barley loaves and two small fish" (6:1-14).

To demonstrate His power over nature, He walked on the water (6:16-24). After that, John wrote, Jesus healed a man who had been blind from his birth (9:1-38). And, in one of His greatest miracles, He brought Lazarus back from the dead—after Lazarus had been in the tomb for four days (11:1-44). All of these miraculous signs "are written that you may believe that Jesus is the Christ, the Son of God, and that by believing you may have life in His name" (20:31).

The Apostle John also wrote that "Jesus did many other signs [other than these seven miracles] in the presence of His disciples, which are not recorded in this book" (the Book of John) (20:30). But these seven signs were selected to uniquely demonstrate Christ's deity—that He was one with the Father. And as Dr. Merrill Tenney points out in his commentary on the fourth Gospel, "Each of these signs revealed some specific characteristic of Jesus' power and person" (*John: The Gospel of Belief*. Eerdmans, 1953, pp. 30-31).

When Jesus changed the water into wine, it was the *best* wine, demonstrating He was the Master of *quality*. When He healed the nobleman's son, while the boy was more than 20 miles away, He showed He was the Master of *distance or space*. When He instantaneously healed the impotent man who had been crippled for 38 years, He demonstrated that He was the Master of *time*.

Then when He miraculously fed the 5,000 (besides women and children), He demonstrated He was the Master of *quantity*. When He walked on the water, He demonstrated He was the Master of *natural law*. When He healed the man who had been born blind, He demonstrated He was the Master over *misfortune*. And finally, when He raised Lazarus from the dead, He demonstrated He was Master over *death*.

It is obvious why John selected these seven miracles. Each one points dramatically to the fact that Jesus Christ is who He claimed to be—God in the flesh. This was why John began his Gospel by coming right to the point. "In the beginning was the Word, and the Word was with God, and the Word was God. He was with God in the beginning. Through Him all things were made; without Him nothing was made that has been made. . . . The Word became flesh and lived for a while among us. We have seen His glory, the glory of the one and only Son, who came from the Father, full of grace and truth" (1:1-3, 14).

A New Kind of Miracle

Jesus claimed to be God and demonstrated that fact with a variety of signs and miracles. But now in His high priestly prayer, He asked for a new kind of sign to demonstrate to the world that He was from God—the miracle of oneness and unity among His followers. He would no longer be visibly present to personally demonstrate His deity, as He had been for three-and-one-half years. But He was leaving behind a small group of men who, through their unity, would demonstrate their relationship to Jesus Christ. Throughout the centuries it was God's plan that Christians everywhere emulate Christ.

Dr. Francis Schaeffer has called this unity "the final apologetic." No amount of intellectual argumentation to prove the deity of Christ will ever be able to replace the reality of Christianity flowing through Christians who are in proper relationship with one another. Interestingly, Christians are to judge whether or not people are true Christians by *what* they believe—their doctrine (1 John 2:20-23). Anyone who denied that Jesus was the Christ and from God could not be classified as a true believer. But the world is to judge Christianity by *the way Christians live*—their love and their fruit—all of which reflects itself in unity and oneness. Inherent in this dynamic is miraculous power to convince unbelievers that Christ is one with God, making this unity possible (*The Church at the End of the Twentieth Century*. InterVarsity Press, 1970, p. 139).

Maintaining Unity

Christ prayed for unity among His followers. But unity is not automatic. Satan's primary attack on believers has been to destroy oneness. This is clear from church history.

People everywhere are searching for acceptance and love. The heart of every living person cries out for it. So Satan attempts to create a false "oneness" among people who are not true Christians.

He wants to destroy unity among *true* Christians. In this way, non-Christians will not be attracted to doctrinally pure Christianity. At the same time, Satan tries to enhance cults that propagate false doctrines—particularly false views regarding Christ's deity. Unfortunately, this method of securing "disciples" works. And Satan knows this more keenly than we do.

I know of one young woman who was attracted to Sun Myung Moon's Unification Church. The reason? She felt loved and accepted, and sensed a oneness of purpose among these people—something she evidently did not sense in her home or in the church she had attended from childhood. And once she was in the movement, no amount of "sound doctrine" could convince her that these people were in violation of Scripture. Having her emotional needs met was far more important to her than intellectual arguments regarding the deity of Christ.

But this need not happen. Christ—*who is God*—prayed for us. It is possible for Christians to maintain unity *and* to attract non-Christians to the Son of God. If superficial unity attracts non-Christians to a movement that denies Christ's power, how much more will true unity attract unbelievers to an accurate view of Christ? This was why Paul exhorted the Ephesians to "make every effort to keep the unity of the Spirit through the bond of peace" (Eph. 4:3).

Unity and the Contemporary Church

How can unity be maintained among Christians today? Since it is possible, what steps must be taken?

1. Realize that Christ was praying for "observable" unity. Some people believe that Christ's prayer in John 17 was referring to the mystical union that exists in the "invisible church." They believe that true unity exists among all Christians of all time, and they believe that these people are known only to God Himself. This interpretation, however, makes Christ's prayer illogical and nonsensical. It *is* possible for Christians to experience unity while on earth. Furthermore, it is possible for the world to *see* our unity.

Christ was not referring to the *positional unity* which exists among all true Christians, whether or not we are properly related to one another in our daily activities. Rather, Christ was praying for an observable, practical, and experiential oneness that can only exist where Christians are gathered together in flesh-and-blood relationships. Where true Christians are gathered, they are to demonstrate this unity so the world can learn of Christ and what He has done for all mankind on the Cross.

It is only logical then to conclude that He was referring to local groups of believers which we call churches. Usually New Testament believers lived in one geographical area and their relationships with one another were visible to non-Christians in that particular community. The pagans in Ephesus could not see the Christians in Thessalonica. Nor could the non-Christians in Thessalonica see the believers in Ephesus. And so it is today. Every local body of believers that meets together regularly should demonstrate a oneness of heart and mind and spirit so that non-Christians in that area will know who Jesus Christ is.

From this conclusion, we see that Christ was not referring to ecumenical unity. There is certainly a true ecumenism where born again Christians can cooperate on a wider basis than with a local church. But generally speaking, the world cannot *see* this kind of love and unity. The oneness that Christ prayed for was that day-to-day phenomenon that can permeate and penetrate a geographical area over a period of time. Jesus Christ primarily had in mind local churches.

2. *Realize that the basic cause of disunity is pride and selfishness.* In the Upper Room, the disciples each wanted a position of authority over the others. They were unwilling to serve one another. Their root problem was pride and selfishness.

Paul spoke of this problem in his letters. When dealing with the lack of unity in various local churches in the New Testament world, he consistently pinpointed pride and selfishness as a basic *cause*—and advocated humility as a *cure*.

This is best illustrated with the Corinthians, who had more divisions among them than any other New Testament church. In chapter 12 of 1 Corinthians, Paul carefully illustrated spiritual oneness by using the example of the human body. No member of the physical body can boast that it does not need other members of that body. And so the same is true in the body of Christ—His church. We all need one another. We cannot think we are more important than others. If we do, we will destroy the unity that Christ prayed for.

Before dealing with the subject of unity in the body of Christ in his Ephesian letter, Paul laid down the same basic ground rule for maintaining this unity. "Be completely humble and gentle; be patient, bearing with one another in love" (Eph. 4:2).

Furthermore, we see the same emphasis in his letter to the Roman Christians. Just prior to the section dealing with unity in the body, he again spoke of humility as a basic ingredient in creating *body oneness*. He wrote, "For by the grace given me I say to every one of you: do not think of yourself more highly than you ought, but rather think of yourself with sober judgment, in accordance with the measure of faith God has given you. Just as each of us has one body with many members, and these members do not all have the same function, so in Christ we who are many form one body, and each member belongs to all the others" (Rom. 12:3-5).

And again, we must realize that it is only as we maintain this attitude that Christ's prayer for unity will be answered.

Practical Steps for Maintaining Unity

The steps for maintaining unity in the church today are in essence the same as those given to the first-century church. They are probably best outlined in the "one another" injunctions—particularly those stated by the Apostle Paul. Following are 10 such exhortations that, when practiced, will lead to unity. (For more in-depth study of these commands, see Dr. Getz' book *Building Up One Another*, published by Victor.)

1. "Be devoted to one another in brotherly love" (Rom. 12:10a).

2. "Honor one another above yourselves" (Rom. 12:10b).

3. "Be of the same mind with one another" (Rom. 15:5, NASB).

4. "Accept one another, then, just as Christ accepted you" (Rom. 15:7).

5. "Serve one another in love" (Gal. 5:13).

6. "Carry each other's burdens" (Gal. 6:2).

7. "Submit to one another out of reverence for Christ" (Eph. 5:21).

8. "Bear with each other and forgive whatever grievances you may have against one another" (Col. 3:13).

9. "Encourage one another and build each other up" (1 Thes. 5:11).

10. "Offer hospitality to one another without grumbling" (1 Peter 4:9).

A Personal Response

Looking back over these practical "one another" injunctions, check any you are presently violating. Think of specific individuals involved. For example, you can think of relationships with other Christians where you are honoring yourself above them? Are there any Christians you cannot accept because of purely cultural differences? Is there any Christian who has hurt you and whom you have not forgiven?

Determine with God's help that you will correct any situation that is in violation of His will and that is interfering with the unity and oneness that should exist between you and another Christian.

Before completing this personal assignment, however, think carefully about these words penned by Dr. Francis Schaeffer:

In our own groups, in our own closed Christian communities, even in our families, when we have shown lack of love toward another, we as Christians do not just automatically go and say we are sorry. On even the very simplest level, it is never very easy.

It may sound simplistic to start with saying we are sorry and asking forgiveness, but it is not. This is the way of renewed fellowship, whether it is between a husband and wife, a parent and child, within a Christian community, or between groups. When we have shown lack of love toward the other, we are called by God to go and say, "I'm sorry. . . . I really am sorry."

If I'm not willing to say "I'm sorry" when I have wronged somebody else—especially when I have not loved him—I have not even started to think about the meaning of the Christian oneness which the world can see. The world has a right to question whether I am a Christian. And more than that, let me say it again, if I'm not willing to do this very simple thing, the world has a right to question whether Jesus was sent from God and whether Christianity is true (*The Church at the End of the Twentieth Century*, p. 139).

You yourselves are our letter, written on our hearts, known and read by everybody.

2 Corinthians 3:2

6

Attracting People to Christ

Some who have read the letters written to the New Testament churches have concluded they say very little, if anything, about evangelism. They see their purpose as primarily edification.

In a sense, they are correct. These letters *were* written to build up the body of Christ. But the reason these people conclude that the epistles have little or nothing to say about evangelism is that they don't understand God's total plan for winning lost people to Christ. They have defined evangelism basically as a personal and individual responsibility. In a future chapter we'll explore more completely why this has happened.

Don't misunderstand. Winning the lost to Christ *is* a personal responsibility. But God never intended that individual witness be separated from corporate witness. In fact, it is corporate or "body" evangelism that makes personal evangelism natural (not forced) and truly productive (creating lasting results).

The reason many Christians miss the evangelistic emphasis in the New Testament epistles is that they have never clearly understood Christ's teachings in chapters 13, 15, and 17 of the Book of John.

Let's review.

• In John 13 the Lord instructed His followers to "love one another" so that all men would know they are His disciples.

• In John 15 He told them it would bring glory to His Father if they bore much fruit, showing themselves to be His disciples.

• In John 17 He prayed for His 11 disciples (and us) that they (and we) might "be brought to complete unity to let the world know" why He sent Christ into this world.

These three ideas form a powerful concept that serves as a key in understanding the evangelistic thrust in the New Testament epistles. True, these letters were written to help Christians grow spiritually. But inseparably interwoven into the instructions to grow in Christ is the outworking of what Christ taught His disciples in the Upper Room; what He illustrated as He walked by the grape arbor; and what He said to His Father as He stood and prayed for Christians of all time.

This forms a backdrop for understanding such statements as those made by Paul to the Corinthians. "You yourselves [as a *body* of believers in Corinth] are our letter written on our hearts, known and read by everybody. You show that you are a letter from Christ, the result of our ministry, written not with ink but with the Spirit of the living God, not on tablets of stone but on tablets of human hearts" (2 Cor. 3:2-3).

Here Paul contrasted the Old Covenant, the "old commandment" we discussed in chapter 1, with the New Covenant (3:6). The Old Covenant (the Law) condemned man. Though it seemed harsh and cruel, it drove men to seek relief for the burden of their sins. It prepared people for the coming of Jesus Christ, who then instituted a "new commandment" that would not drive people to Christ, but that would *attract* them to Christ. Thus, Paul said, "The letter [the old law] kills, but the Spirit gives life" (3:6).

But let's look further at how the epistles in the New Testament clarify what Christ taught in John 13, 15 and 17. Following are three lists of injunctions given by New Testament writers that demonstrate clearly the evangelistic thrust in the epistles. Keep in mind, however, that these three sections form a unifying concept, just as John 13 to 17 develops a basic theme. Jesus was developing a unified truth. *Love, holiness,* and *unity* are interrelated. They're only listed in separate categories in these chapters in order to show the relationship between Christ's statement to His disciples as recorded by John and the emphasis in the rest of the New Testament.

Christ's Command to "Love One Another"

In the Old Testament God's primary means for drawing people to Himself was through the commandments He gave to Moses. These laws condemned men and made them aware of their sins. They also drove people to seek a *means* of forgiveness. God provided a temporary means at Mount Sinai—a system of sacrifices given to Israel to provisionally atone for sin. But in the New Testament, God gave a *new* commandment of love (John 13:34-35). And it was love that would reveal to all men the one and final sacrifice for sin—Jesus Christ Himself.

This unique and divine strategy for communicating the love of Christ is confirmed again and again in the letters that were written to the various New Testament churches. Note the following injunctions to "love one another." (This is a selective list. We are commanded to love one another thoughout the New Testament.)

• "Be devoted to one another in brotherly love" (Rom. 12:10).

• "Keep on loving each other as brothers" (Heb. 13:1).

• "Love your neighbor as yourself" (James 2:8).

• "Love each other deeply because love covers a multitude of sins" (1 Peter 4:8).

• "Since God so loved us, we also ought to love one another" (1 John 4:11).

• "Love never fails" (1 Cor. 13:8).

• "Be patient, bearing with one another in love" (Eph. 4:2).

• "And this is my prayer: that your love may abound more and more" (Phil. 1:9).

• "Be encouraged in heart and united in love" (Col. 2:2).

• "May the Lord make your love increase" (1 Thes. 3:12).

Against the backdrop of Christ's new commandment to His disciples in John 13, it is very clear from these injunctions that God's plan is to convey His love through His people. Peter and John particularly, as they penned their letters, were simply reporting what Christ had told them in the Upper Room. And Paul, following his conversion, gained these insights by direct revelation from God Himself. Love in the body of Christ is the means to convey God's love to non-Christians.

But as we've already seen, loving one another involves more than kind and gracious relational experiences. It involves holy and righteous relationships. And this leads us to what Christ stated in John 15.

Christ's Command to "Bear Much Fruit"
Love involves concern for one another, but it also involves a total Christian life-style that permeates our relationships with others. "This is to My Father's glory, that you bear much fruit, showing yourselves to be My disciples" (John 15:8). Again we see this concept confirmed throughout the New Testament epistles.

• "So whether you eat or drink or whatever you do, do it all for the glory of God. Do not cause anyone to stumble, whether Jews, Greeks, or the Church of God" (1 Cor. 10:31-32).

• "Live as children of light (for the fruit of the light consists in all goodness, righteousness, and truth)" (Eph. 5:8-9).

• "Be wise in the way you act toward outsiders" (Col. 4:5).

• "Live peaceful and quiet lives in all godliness and holiness. This is good, and pleases God our Saviour, who wants all men to be saved and to come to the knowledge of the truth" (1 Tim. 2:2-4).

• "Always be prepared to give an answer to everyone who asks you to give the reason for the hope that you have" (1 Peter 3:15).

The intended evangelistic impact of the "fruit of righteousness" as lived out by a loving body of Christians is very obvious in these biblical statements. Correlated with the previous statements on "loving one another," they help us to see what Christ had in mind when He said, "This is to My Father's glory, that you bear much fruit, showing yourselves to be My disciples" (John 15:8).

But the capstone—the real visible aspect of Christ's two injunctions and the result of that visibility—is seen in His prayer for unity among believers. Loving one another and bearing fruit were to provide the foundation for this unity.

Christ's Prayer for Unity

Christ's prayer for unity clearly involved "the world"—those who do not know Christ. His desire is that unbelievers see unity and oneness among Christians and, in turn, discover that Jesus Christ is the God-Man, the only true Saviour of the world. "May they be brought to complete unity to let the world know that You sent Me and have loved them even as You have loved Me" (John 17:23).

Again, we see this emphasis confirmed in the epistles. Note the references to harmony, peace, agreeing, avoiding divisions, being like-minded, being one.

• "Live in harmony with one another" (Rom. 12:16).

• "Make every effort to do what leads to peace" (Rom. 14:19).

• "May the God who gives endurance and encouragement give you a spirit of unity among yourselves as you follow Christ Jesus, so that with one heart and mouth you may glorify the God and Father of our Lord Jesus Christ" (Rom. 15:5-6).

• "I appeal . . . that all of you agree with one another so that there may be no divisions among you and that you may be perfectly united in mind and thought" (1 Cor. 1:10).

• "Make every effort to keep the unity of the Spirit in the bond of peace" (Eph. 4:3).

• "Make my joy complete by being like-minded, having the same love, being one in spirit and purpose" (Phil. 2:2).

Implications for Evangelism Today

What does all of this mean to us?

1. We must recognize that Satan attempts to destroy love and unity in our local churches. This has been part of his diabolical scheme to keep non-Christians from observing what Christ prayed for in John 17. Satan hates the message of the incarnation and the deity of Christ. And this is understandable, for it is the essence of Christianity. Without this truth, Christianity would merely be another religion.

2. Satan attempts to create a worldly mentality in the church—to lead us into materialism, immorality, and legalism. *Materialism* among Christians destroys faith, and often causes resentment among non-Christians. *Immorality* deceives and disillusions people and drives them away from Christ. And *legalism* focuses on externals, turning people away from true holiness and Christlike attitudes and behavior. On the contrary, true righteousness in a local body of believers becomes a dynamic force to convict non-Christians of their sins and to turn them toward Christ, the One who can forgive them.

3. Christians must recognize that God's evangelistic methodology in the New Testament is more than going. It involves being. And it involves developing contemporary strategies to expose non-Christians to the realities of Christianity. It means taking to the world not just the words of the Gospel but also the incarnate Christ embodied in "the functioning church."

It also means creating an environment, when the church assembles, that will *attract* the world—not drive it away. True, people may be offended by the message of the Cross, but let it never be said that they are offended by inconsistent Christian behavior. Unfortunately, many non-Christians are offended, not by the Cross per se, but by the *way* Christians present the message of the Cross. And even more offensive is a church that portrays disharmony, disunity, and a lack of love. This is devastating to effective evangelism.

4. This kind of evangelistic function involves the total body of Christ in the process of evangelism and edification. So many people today are caught up in a guilt trap because they personally have difficulty winning people to Christ. But everyone who is involved in contributing to love and unity is also involved in carrying out the Great Commission.

This does not release Christians from the responsibility to personally share Christ. But it does put personal evangelism in a much broader context—a context that sets the stage for personal witnessing that is natural and very fruitful. In a real sense, this kind of personal sharing is confirmed by a miracle—the miracle of unity that Christ prayed for—the miracle that will demonstrate that Jesus Christ has come from God to save the world.

Let me illustrate. A man approached me one day and told me he wasn't sure he was a Christian. "I've attended church all my life," he said. "In fact, I've served as an officer in several churches. But I'm not sure I know what the Christian life is all about."

Because of his schedule, we weren't able to continue the conversation. However, we met the next day in my office. And when he walked in, his first comments were *not* about my sermons.

This man had been impressed with the people he had come to know—the people who made up the church I was pastoring. "I've never experienced anything like this before," he said, with a note of intensity in his voice. "These people really care about each other. There's real love here." And then he said, "I'm convinced that I'm really not a Christian. But I want to be."

I had the privilege of leading this man to know Jesus Christ personally. But I only "drew the net." It was really every member of that local body of believers who brought him to Christ. It was *their* love, *their* unity, *their* Christian attitudes, and *their* behavior that had convinced him that he should do something about it. This is the miracle Christ prayed for.

A Personal Response

It is very clear from Scripture that God's plan to bring men to Himself involves people. He uses people to reach people.

To what extent are you willing to be a dynamic part of the body of Christ? Many Christians are so influenced by the "individualistic" type of thinking that permeates our culture that they allow it to affect their commitment to and involvement in Christ's body—the church. Perhaps you need to make a new commitment to love others in the body, demonstrate the fruit of righteousness, and strive to create oneness and unity.

Following are some specific ways you can do this. Select the one that is the most appropriate to your life and make a new commitment. Set it up as a goal and apply it to your life immediately.

• I will be present regularly when the body meets—whether as a total group or in small groups.

• I will reach out to people in the body, particularly visitors.

• I will evaluate all of my actions in the light of Scripture to make sure that I am contributing to a corporate reflection of God's righteousness.

• I will make every effort to be a peacemaker—to always "speak the truth in love" and to do all I can to "build up others."

• I will be ready to participate in any way I can to be a part of the evangelistic outreach of my church to neighbors, friends, and non-Christians wherever our lives touch.

Therefore go and make disciples of all nations.
Matthew 28:19

7

Making Disciples

The events of Christ's life on earth began to culminate rather quickly following His Upper Room discourse. After His prayer to the Father for oneness and unity among His disciples, He crossed the Kidron Valley with the men and entered an olive grove, a place where He had often met with them. And it was there that Judas, who knew the place well, betrayed the Lord.

Fear gripped the disciples (as Christ had predicted) and, even though they had believed in Him as the Messiah, they all forsook Him (John 16:32). But later, they gathered together to mourn what was, from their perspective, a tragic event and to try to make sense out of what had happened.

Even at this juncture they did not fully understand God's plan for His Son and for them. Their hearts were filled with intense fear of their fellow Jews who had called for Christ's death. And to make their lives even more miserable, their hearts must have burned with shame for their own unfaithfulness. Peter, of all men, probably felt the most distress, for he had boasted that he would never forsake the Lord.

But even though they had been unfaithful to Him, He had not forsaken them. After His death and resurrection, while they were gathered together in a room with the doors locked, Jesus suddenly appeared. He stood in their midst, calming their anxiety. "Peace be with you," He said. He reassured them that He was indeed the Christ by showing them His pierced hands and side.

In the context of this reassurance He also restated His plans for them. "As the Father has sent Me," He said, "I am sending you" (20:21). He was continuing the same message He had been teaching them before the Cross, in the Upper Room, by the grape arbor, and on their way to the garden where He had been captured.

Christ's death and resurrection were necessary in order to make the Gospel message complete and powerful. He was born to die and to be raised again from the dead (Acts 2:22-24). There was no other way. For this purpose He came into the world. As Paul wrote to the Corinthians, without Christ's death and resurrection there would be no message of hope and eternal life (1 Cor. 15:3-8; 12-14).

Christ's Final Days on Earth

Following His resurrection, Jesus appeared to His disciples "over a period of 40 days" (Acts 1:3). During these appearances He had a two-fold purpose: to convince His followers that He was indeed alive, and to commission them to carry this Good News to the ends of the earth. Luke recorded that He "gave many convincing proofs that He was alive" (1:3) and several years later Paul wrote that "He appeared to Peter, and then to the Twelve. After that, He appeared to more than 500 of the brothers at the same time" (1 Cor. 15:5-6).

The Great Commission, as we've come to call it, is recorded in one form or another in all four Gospel accounts. In various settings and in various ways Jesus stated and restated His concern that the Gospel should be shared with all people. But no statement rings with more clarity than what He said to the disciples on the mountain in Galilee, probably near the end of the 40 days. "All authority in heaven and on earth has been given to Me. Therefore go and make disciples of all nations, baptizing them in the name of the Father and of the Son and of the Holy

Spirit, and teaching them to obey everything I have commanded you. And surely I will be with you always, to the very end of the age" (Matt. 28:18b-20).

Note one very important observation. Christ told these men to *"go and make disciples"*; that is, to produce other believers. There is an important assumption we frequently overlook when we read this Commission. What Christ had already said to His men in the Upper Room, what He had said while they passed the grape arbor, and what He had asked in His high priestly prayer all laid the foundation for the Great Commission.

When Christ told these men to make disciples, He wanted those whom they taught to realize from these men's lives that they *were* what they were trying to reproduce in others—*disciples of the Lord Jesus Christ*. They were, as a *group*, to convey the reality of the Gospel with their lives as they communicated the Gospel message with their words.

When we look at what Christ taught about evangelism, we clearly see that He emphasized to His followers that they could not make disciples effectively unless they first demonstrated what a disciple was. Furthermore, no individual disciple could adequately convey that visual message alone. It would take *disciples*—loving one another as a unified body—to demonstrate God's love visually. This would give the verbal message authenticity and make it believable.

This combination—the visual and the verbal—would make a tremendous impact on the unbeliever. Though non-Christians might not grasp all that was involved, because of a God-created need in their hearts for acceptance and love, they *would* be impressed by what they saw and experienced. Not all unbelievers would respond in faith. But most people are looking for unconditional acceptance and for the chance to share in this kind of community.

The Great Commission's Relevance

In the late 1700s a young man stood up one day in a meeting of ministers in Northampton, England, and innocently suggested that they have a discussion about Christ's Commission in Matthew 28:19-20.

"Don't you think," he asked, "that Christ's command given to the apostles to teach all nations is our responsibility too?"

The moderator of the meeting responded with irritation. Calling him a "miserable enthusiast," he snapped, "Young man, sit down! When God pleases to convert the heathen, He will do it without your aid or mine!"

That young man was William Carey. And fortunately, he was not squelched by the minister's insensitivity and personal ignorance. Carey continued to research the Bible, and to personally preach and teach the Gospel to lost people. God blessed his efforts and used him to launch what has come to be recognized as the "Era of Modern Missions."

Unfortunately, many people who claim to be Christians have demonstrated an attitude similar to the moderator's. Usually negative attitudes are far more passive, but they are negative attitudes nevertheless. And this kind of negative outlook shows little or no concern for those who do not know Christ. Many pastors and Christian leaders contentedly minister to a body of believers in a particular area without any emphasis on evangelism and outreach—never reaching their own community or beyond.

I grew up in a church like this. The whole denomination was ingrown in its attitudes and behavior. There was no concern for anyone outside of our own group. Any person who had a vision to share the Gospel of Christ with others was discouraged and even criticized. I faced that kind of criticism, and was eventually excommunicated from the group because of my own evangelistic activities.

I clearly remember visiting the church one Sunday after a long absence. In Sunday School class, I shared an exciting evangelistic experience I had on an Indian reservation in Montana. And that event became the final step leading to my excommunication.

This church claimed to believe the Bible, and members prided themselves in being "God's special people." Yet they strongly opposed sharing the Gospel with others. Unfortunately, many religious groups that deny the deity of Christ and salvation by grace through faith are far more active in promoting their false views than many Christians are who believe the truth.

Disregard for the Great Commission

Why do we ignore the Great Commission? Mainly because we are apathetic and disobedient regarding what Christ taught. Since we are not motivated by a "works" theology, we tend to take advantage of God's grace. If we believed our salvation depended on our witness to others, we'd be very active doing what we believed was necessary to be saved.

However, some people who believe in salvation by grace, apart from works, actually teach that the Great Commission is not relevant today. Some argue that this responsibility was given only to the apostles—not to all Christians. Others teach that the Great Commission involved a "kingdom message" and will be fulfilled by Jewish believers after the church has been removed from the earth.

I cannot accept these arguments for several reasons. First, I do not believe the Bible teaches that the Great Commission was given only to the apostles. It is true that Christ directed many of His statements to them personally. In fact, the "11 disciples" are mentioned specifically in the context of Matthew 28:19-20. (See v. 16.) Later we'll see that the apostles had a special place in God's evangelistic program that was not designed as a standard for believers of all time.

But God's unique plan for them does not invalidate the relevance of the Great Commission to us. In fact, Scripture shows that other believers were also present on occasions when Jesus in essence gave the very same Commission as He gave in Matthew 28:19-20 (see Luke 24:33-49). Furthermore, many others eventually carried the Gospel out from Jerusalem, since some of the apostles stayed close to home base and handled the problems in the expanding church in Jerusalem (Acts 8:1, 4).

Second, I have no difficulty accepting the fact that after Christ comes for the church that the "Gospel of the Kingdom" will be preached to all nations. Furthermore, I believe that the Great Commission in Matthew 28:19-20 includes that plan. But I *do* have difficulty restricting Christ's statements to that interpretation. There are too many other injunctions in Scripture regarding our responsibility to reach the world for Christ that clearly involve believers of all times, not just the Jews.

Taking the Great Commission Seriously

There are several basic reasons for taking the Great Commission seriously. They are theological reasons, and Luke spelled this out clearly in his account of Christ's conversation, not only with the apostles, but also with the other disciples who were with them (Luke 24:33). In this passage there are three theological reasons why we as Christians must take Christ's Commission to heart.

1. Man is sinful and needs a Saviour. In Luke's account of the Great Commission Jesus summarized for the apostles the primary message that appears again and again throughout the Old Testament Scriptures. "Then He opened their minds so they could understand the Scriptures. He told them, 'This is what is written: The Christ will suffer and rise from the dead on the third day, and *repentance* and *forgiveness of sins* will be preached in His name to all nations' " (24:45-47).

All people are sinners. And we all need forgiveness. This is the message of the Bible and the experience recorded in all human history. And furthermore, it is your experience—if you're honest with yourself and with God. Sin entered human history in the Garden of Eden through the disobedience of Adam and Eve. Since that time, all of us have been affected by its presence, its power, and its results.

Sin is indeed a reality, and any man who denies its existence in his life is deceived. "If we claim to be without sin, we deceive ourselves and the truth is not in us" (1 John 1:8). Paul, summarizing numerous Old Testament references in Romans 3:10-18, put it all together with one concise statement: "For all have sinned and fall short of the glory of God" (3:23).

Dr. George Peters, professor emeritus of world missions at

Dallas Theological Seminary, spoke directly to this issue when he wrote: "Sin is written in bold letters upon the pages of the Bible. Only four chapters are exempt from this evil. According to Genesis 1—2, sin was not a part of original human history. Neither is it found in Revelation 21—22. There is thus a brief pre-sin history (Gen. 1—2) and a post-sin history (Rev. 21—22). The rest of the Bible (Gen. 3—Rev. 20) is a record of human sin and divine intervention, preparation, accomplishment, and actualization of salvation" (*A Biblical Theology of Missions.* Moody Press, 1972, p. 15).

2. Man cannot escape the penalty of sin except through the person and work of Jesus Christ. Note again the Lord's Commission in Luke's Gospel. *"The Christ* will suffer and rise from the dead on the third day, and repentance and forgiveness of sins will be preached *in His name* to all nations" (Luke 24:46-47).

The Old Testament points to Christ's sacrifice at Calvary. This is why Jesus said on that day to His followers, "Everything must be fulfilled that is written about Me in the Law of Moses, the Prophets, and the Psalms" (24:44). Then Christ "opened their minds so they could understand the Scriptures"—that is, the Old Testament Scriptures. And that message involved His death and resurrection so that men might be able to turn from their sins and be forgiven. From Genesis 3:15 onward, that message permeates and interweaves with all the major events recorded in the Old Testament. If we believe the Bible at all, we realize that salvation and forgiveness of sin could come only through the death and resurrection of Jesus Christ. This is indeed the Gospel—the Good News (1 Cor. 15:1-8).

3. Man cannot encounter Christ and experience forgiveness unless he knows who Christ is and what Christ has done. This too is very clear from Luke's account: "The Christ will suffer and rise from the dead on the third day, and repentance and forgiveness of sins *will be preached* in His name to all nations, beginning in Jerusalem. You are *witnesses* of these things" (Luke 24:46-48).

God has chosen to use men and women to spread the Good News of salvation to people who are not Christians, people who are trapped in sin and need to be saved. All those who do not know Christ must pay the penalty for their sins. And they cannot be saved unless they believe in Jesus Christ as their personal Saviour from sin. But they cannot trust Christ unless they *know* what He has done for them. This is another theological reason why the Great Commission is still relevant today.

But there is also an historical reason. Christ has not yet returned. Why? This was a question being asked by a number of people in the New Testament world. Peter spoke to that question directly and deliberately. "But do not forget this one thing, dear friends: with the Lord a day is like a thousand years, and a thousand years are like a day. The Lord is not slow in keeping His promise, as some understand slowness. He is patient with you, not wanting anyone to perish, but everyone to come to repentance" (2 Peter 3:8-9).

Some Personal Questions

How do you evaluate the Great Commission? Do you really believe that people who do not know Christ personally will be eternally separated from God? Do you really believe that He is the only way to heaven?

A subtle religious philosophy is spreading, even among many who claim to be Christians. This philosophy teaches a comfortable universalism. Webster defines *universalism* as "the theological doctrine that all souls will eventually find salvation in the grace of God." In other words, people who believe this philosophy feel that all religions offer salvation, that all religions provide a way to God. To the universalist, Christianity is no different from other beliefs—it's just one more way to God.

One day at the airport I met a young girl who was selling religious books. She was promoti. g an eastern religion. I told her I was a Christian, that I followed Jesus Christ. "Oh, that's all right," she said. "You can follow Him. We follow another religious leader. But they're both saying the same thing."

I reminded her that Jesus said that He was *the* Way and that no man could get to God but by Him.

"That's OK," she said. "That's what He believed, but there are other ways too."

Obviously, this young woman did not know much about Jesus and what He really taught and claimed. As we've seen from our study thus far, we cannot misconstrue His claims, unless we interpret everything He said in a nonrational or figurative way. There is no question what Paul believed.

"He is the image of the invisible God, the firstborn over all creation. For by Him all things were created: things in heaven and on earth, visible and invisible, whether thrones or powers or rulers or authorities; all things were created by Him and for Him. He is before all things, and in Him all things hold together. And He is the head of the body, the church; He is the beginning and the firstborn from among the dead, so that in everything He might have the supremacy. For God was pleased to have all fullness dwell in Him, and through Him to reconcile to Himself all things, whether things on earth or things in heaven, by making peace through His blood, shed on the cross" (Col. 1:15-20).

But on the other hand, this young girl's zeal caused real conviction in my own heart. How concerned am I that others know that Jesus Christ really is the only way to God? How much zeal do I have? True, she had zeal without knowledge. But so often, I must confess, I have knowledge without zeal. What about you?

A Personal Response

Think for a moment about your own experience with Christ. Would you be a Christian today if someone had not loved you and told you about Jesus Christ—a parent, a teacher, a pastor, a friend? Does your own experience say anything to you personally regarding your responsibility to be involved in helping other Christians carry out the Great Commission?

But you will receive power when the Holy Spirit comes on you; and you will be My witnesses in Jerusalem, and in all Judea and Samaria, and to the ends of the earth.

Acts 1:8

8

God's First Evangelistic Plan

When we study any subject in the New Testament, we must carefully determine how that subject related to first-century Christians and how it relates to Christians today. This is particularly true when we study evangelism. If we do not make these distinctions, we can become thoroughly confused, discouraged, or overcome with guilt. Some Christians eventually give up trying to share Christ at all. Often because of this confusion, some Christians equate normal psychological experiences with what the Bible defines as a unique and special experience for selected individuals.

For many years I experienced many of these frustrating emotions. Since becoming a Christian in my teenage years, I have always taken the Bible seriously and have generally had a strong desire to do God's will in every respect. Consequently, if God tells me to do something, I want to obey Him. If He promises me certain things, I want to claim those promises. My basic problem came as I applied certain scriptural statements to my own life when the Lord intended these for a special group of first-century Christians. Jesus Christ never meant for some of His statements and promises to be regarded as the standard for Christians of all time. If we read the Bible carefully, we can clearly see what these things are.

Acts 1:8 is a specific illustration of this. "You will receive power," Jesus said, "when the Holy Spirit comes on you; and you will be My witnesses in Jerusalem, and in all Judea and Samaria, and to the ends of the earth."

Many well-meaning Christians believe that they have been endowed with the power Jesus referred to in this verse. But, you say, isn't that what Jesus said? Yes, it is, but let's take a closer look at *what* Jesus said, to *whom* He said it, and what He really *meant*. And more specifically, what did He actually mean by the word *power*?

Let's look carefully at the context in which Jesus made this statement, noting particularly how the word *power* (*dunamis*) is used in the New Testament and particularly in the Book of Acts.

The Meaning of God's Power

The author of the Book of Hebrews gave us a specific key for unlocking the meaning of God's power mentioned by Jesus in Acts 1:8. He succinctly summarized God's redemptive strategy in chapter 2, following a profound and provocative question: "How shall we escape if we ignore such a great salvation? This salvation, which was first announced by the Lord, was confirmed to us by those who heard Him. God also testified to it [this salvation] by signs, wonders, and various miracles, and gifts of the Holy Spirit distributed according to His will" (Heb. 2:3-4).

In these two verses we have a brief but comprehensive outline describing God's evangelistic methods for launching the church. Biblical history fills in the details, particularly as it is recorded in the Gospels and in the Book of Acts. Following is that outline as it emerges from the scriptural text.

1. "This salvation . . . was first announced by the Lord." Most of what is referred to here by the author of Hebrews is recorded in the Gospels. Four New Testament witnesses— Matthew, Mark, Luke, and John—have given us a dramatic record of Christ's life on this earth. Mostly devoted to His three-and-one-half-year ministry, the Gospel accounts record Christ's message of hope and salvation—that He is indeed the

Saviour of the world. Perhaps His message is best summarized in His prayer to the Father. "Now this is eternal life: that men may know You, the only true God, and Jesus Christ, whom You have sent" (John 17:3).

2. *"This salvation . . . was confirmed to us by those who heard Him."* It is primarily in the Gospels we discover the message of salvation which was "first announced by the Lord." But it is in the Book of Acts that we see this message "confirmed to us by those who heard Him." In the Gospel accounts we find a group of men who again and again heard Him proclaim this message. In the Book of Acts we see them confirming that message to others. In the Gospels they were comprehending, accepting, and believing that message. In the Book of Acts, they devoted themselves to reproducing that believing process in others. Peter included this idea in his sermon in Acts 2: "God has raised this Jesus to life, and we are all *witnesses* of the fact" (Acts 2:32).

3. *"God also testified to it* [this salvation] *by signs, wonders, and various miracles,* [powerful deeds] *and gifts of the Holy Spirit distributed according to His will.* Not only did people believe in Christ because of His message, but also because of His miraculous power. In fact, the word "miracles" in Hebrews 2:4 is translated from the same basic Greek word, *dunamis,* used in Acts 1:8 and translated "power." This is the same word from which we get our word "dynamite." In other words, when Jesus told His followers they would "receive power" to witness for Him (1:8), He was referring to a supernatural ability to work miracles. And as you read through the Gospels and the Book of Acts with this in mind, you realize that this is what Jesus (and the author of Hebrews) had in mind. Let's examine the evidence.

Christ's Miracles
We've already noted in a previous chapter the miracles and signs Jesus performed and how they confirmed His deity. But note what Matthew recorded. "Then Jesus began to denounce the cities in which most of His *miracles* [that is, "powerful deeds"]

had been performed, because they did not repent. 'Woe to you, Chorazin! Woe to you, Bethsaida! If the *miracles* that were performed in you had been performed in Tyre and Sidon, they would have repented long ago in sackcloth and ashes. . . . If the *miracles* that were performed in you had been performed in Sodom, it would have remained to this day'' (Matt. 11:20-21, 23b).

Here again the word "miracles" comes from the basic word *dunamis*, which is translated "power" in Acts 1:8. Peter also testified to this fact once Christ had returned to heaven. "Men of Israel, listen to this: Jesus of Nazareth was a man accredited by God to you by *miracles, wonders and signs,* which God did among you through Him, as you yourselves know" (2:22).

Peter's statement here directly parallels what the author of Hebrews wrote (Heb. 2:4). We see the same correlation in Peter's first sermon to the Gentiles in Acts 10: "You know what has happened throughout Judea, beginning in Galilee after the baptism that John preached—how God anointed Jesus of Nazareth with the Holy Spirit and power, [*dunamis*] and how He went around doing good and healing all who were under the power of the devil, because God was with Him" (Acts 10:37-38).

The Apostles' Miracles

God's evangelistic strategy in launching the church not only involved the powerful deeds performed by Christ, but also "signs, wonders and various miracles" performed by His followers. For a period of time at least, the same power Christ had was transferred to "those who heard Him," which primarily meant the apostles, but not exclusively. And this, it seems, is what Jesus meant when He said, "But you will receive *power* when the Holy Spirit comes on you" (1:8).

When Jesus made this statement He was referring primarily to the apostles (1:2). In fact, the ability to work miracles was a sign of being a true apostle. Thus, in defending his own apostleship, Paul said, "The things that mark an apostle—*signs, wonders and miracles*—were done among you with great perseverance" (2 Cor. 12:12).

Immediately following the Day of Pentecost we see this phenomenon verified. Peter and John healed a crippled beggar at the temple gate in Jerusalem. Those who witnessed this miracle as well as those who just heard about it, "were filled with wonder and amazement." They ran to find Peter and John. And when they found them, Peter asked them, "Men of Israel, why does this surprise you? Why do you stare at us as if by our own power [*dunamis*] or godliness we had made this man walk? The God of Abraham, Isaac, and Jacob, the God of our fathers, has glorified His servant Jesus. . . . We are *witnesses* of this" (Acts 3:12-13, 15). Here again we see a direct fulfillment of what Jesus promised His followers in Acts 1:8—*power* to be His *witnesses*.

But this event was just the beginning. The church continued to grow. "All the believers were one in heart and mind" (Acts 4:32). They even sold their possessions and began to share everything they had with their fellow Christians. We read that "with great *power* the apostles continued to testify to the resurrection of the Lord Jesus" (4:33).

Later when Saul was converted and given the name Paul, he too received this power to affirm his apostleship. Luke recorded that when Paul taught in Ephesus in the "lecture hall of Tyrannus," "God did extraordinary *miracles* [powerful deeds] through him. Handkerchiefs and aprons that had touched him were taken to the sick, and their illnesses were cured and the evil spirits left them" (19:11-12).

There are also significant references to this power in Paul's letter to various churches. Note the following:

• I will not venture to speak of anything except what Christ has accomplished through me in leading the Gentiles to obey God by what I have said and done—by the *power* of signs and miracles, through the *power* of the Spirit (Rom. 15:18-19).

• My message and my preaching were not with wise and

persuasive words, but with a demonstration of the Spirit's *power*, so that your faith might not rest on men's wisdom, but on God's *power* (1 Cor. 2:4-5).

• Does God give you His Spirit and work *miracles* among you because you observe the law, or because you believe what you heard? (Gal. 3:5)

• Brothers loved by God, we know that He has chosen you, because our gospel came to you not simply with words, but also with *power*, with the Holy Spirit and with deep conviction (1 Thes. 1:4-5).

Miracles Performed by Others

This power was not given only to the apostles, but also to other believers God chose to bear special witness of the Resurrection. Two men are mentioned early in the Book of Acts—Stephen and Philip. Both were initially chosen to help take care of the widows in Jerusalem, but soon they were preaching and bearing witness by performing miracles. Luke described Stephen as "a man full of God's grace and *power* [*dunamis*]," which enabled him to perform "great wonders and miraculous signs among the people" (Acts 6:8).

Unfortunately (from a human prospective), Stephen was martyred because of his strong and dynamic witness. Because of the firm witness of other believers, a wave of persecution began. Most of the believers, except the apostles, "were scattered throughout Judea and Samaria" (8:1). One of those who left Jerusalem was Philip. He "went down to a city in Samaria" and preached Christ. Then we read that "when the crowds heard Philip and saw the *miraculous signs* he did, they all paid close attention to what he said" (8:6). In other words, God was testifying to the message of salvation by "signs, wonders, and various miracles."

In fact, a magician named Simon, through trickery and deceit, had conned the people in Samaria into believing that he had great power from God (8:10). But Simon also "followed Philip everywhere, astonished by the great signs and miracles he saw" (8:13). Since Simon's own "powers" were probably based on human skill, he was astonished at what appeared to be magic far beyond anything he had ever known or used personally.

Barnabas was another man who was given special power even though he was not an apostle in the primary sense. In fact, he became one of Paul's first missionary companions. Together, they "spent considerable time" in Iconium, "speaking boldly for the Lord, who confirmed the messages of His grace by enabling them to do *miraculous signs and wonders*" (14:3).

In summary, we see that the "power" Jesus referred to in Acts 1:8 was a special power. It was given to certain Christians, particularly the apostles, to confirm the Gospel message. This was part of God's evangelistic plan to launch the church.

Additional Observations

1. This pattern harmonizes with God's overall method in reaching out in love to lost humanity. God has always been concerned that people have sufficient evidence to know that He is communicating with them. This was true when He called the Children of Israel out of Egypt. After they had spent over 400 years in a pagan culture, and after years of basic "silence" on God's part, He spoke directly to Moses through a burning bush. He then sent Moses back to Egypt with miraculous powers to convince His chosen people that He was their God and that He would deliver them (Ex. 4:1-9).

God verified His message even further with the 10 plagues, the parting of the Red Sea, and His "thunderings" from Mount Sinai. He left no question but that He was God and that He was speaking. He did not expect them to walk by blind faith.

Jesus launched the church in basically the same way. "In the past God spoke . . . through the prophets at many times and in various ways, but in these last days He has spoken to us by His Son" (Heb. 1:1-2). He confirmed Christ's message with "signs, wonders and various miracles"; and He confirmed the message of "those who heard Him" with many of the same "signs, wonders and various miracles" (2:3-4). But once the church was launched these supernatural powers and manifestations began to cease.

2. *Even though God's power was always available to Christ, it was not always used.* It may be surprising that this was true even in Jesus Christ's life while He was on earth. One day when He was speaking in a town in Galilee, many people came to hear Him teach. Luke specifically mentioned that in this instance "the power of the Lord was present for Him to heal the sick" (Luke 5:17). In this case, Jesus chose to direct His supernatural powers to heal others. These special powers were always present in Christ, although sometimes He chose not to use them (Matt. 26:53).

For the apostles, God's power was available only when God chose to reveal it. This was true even before Jesus was crucified. On one occasion Jesus called the disciples together and "gave them power and authority to drive out all demons and to cure diseases" (Luke 9:1). This power was evidently retracted when they returned from this evangelistic tour (v. 10). But they received it once again on the Day of Pentecost when the Holy Spirit came upon them.

Some Practical Questions

1. *Wasn't the Holy Spirit promised to all Christians? And wasn't this power associated with His presence?* Yes, the Holy Spirit *is* promised to all Christians (Acts 2:38). Paul reminded the Corinthians that all Christians are "baptized by one Spirit into one body" (1 Cor. 12:13). However, the fact that God's power was associated with the coming of His Spirit at Pentecost and the "filling of the Spirit" on other occasions in the Book of Acts does not mean that this power is always manifested today, just as it was not always manifested in previous times.

The fact that *all* New Testament believers did not have this unique power demonstrates that it is not automatically associated with the Holy Spirit's presence in a believer's life. He was *always* present in their lives, but He did not always manifest His power overtly and in phenomenal ways; that is, by signs, wonders, and miracles.

We should note that during most of our religious history God has been silent. If we count the years when God in a concentrated way revealed Himself through signs, wonders, and miracles, it would be no more than 150 years out of approximately 4,000 years of religious history.

However, God *has* been present in believers' lives, particularly since Pentecost. On several occasions, Jesus promised that He would *never* leave His followers. But He never promised them (not even the apostles) that they would always have power to work miracles in His name.

2. Isn't this some kind of strange dispensational teaching? No. Extreme dispensationalism advocates that God's message and method of salvation have changed through the centuries. That I cannot accept. Man has always been saved by faith apart from works (even in the Old Testament) and always will be. But God's *ways* and methods of reaching mankind with the salvation message *have* changed.

3. Does God reveal His power today? Remember that God can reveal His power anytime He wants. He could allow His Holy Spirit to come upon people in such a way that they could do the very same things the apostles did. But should this kind of phenomenal event be regarded as a *normative* experience for us? Based on biblical and church history, I do not believe so.

Though God can and does do things that are contrary to natural laws, what is happening today is much different, at least in degree, from what happened among New Testament believers. In some instances, modern Christians may be substituting *natural* psychological and physiological experiences for what were, in New Testament days, *supernatural* spiritual experiences that involved special power from God. In fact, evidence demonstrates that it is very easy to psychologically and physiologically simulate (and sincerely so) what the Bible calls miraculous experiences.

On the other hand, God *is* revealing His power today in a very special way. In fact, He reveals His ongoing power every time a person responds to the Gospel and becomes a Christian. Note what Paul said: "I am not ashamed of the Gospel, because it is the *power* of God for the salvation of everyone who believes" (Rom. 1:16).

But there is another dimension to His power. Though God is not generally confirming His message to the world by enabling certain individuals to perform miracles, He does reveal His power through unified Christians who love one another. Christ's prayer for unity among believers was not only for the apostles, but for all who would believe "through their message" (John 17:20). But for what purpose? To confirm that Jesus was indeed from God, and that He had died and rose again for the sins of the world (17:21, 23).

In some miraculous way God releases the Holy Spirit's power through Christians who are joined together by love. This is indeed a miracle—it conflicts with all psychological laws. People, because of their inborn selfishness, do not seek oneness with others. Rather, they want to meet their own personal needs.

But Christians are to have a different perspective. "Do nothing out of selfish ambition or vain conceit, but in humility consider others better than yourselves. Each of you should look not only to your own interests, but also to the interests of others" (Phil. 2:3-4). With an outlook like this, Christians will make an impact on the world that is indeed miraculous.

A Personal Response

Perhaps you have been confused about God's power as mentioned in Acts 1:8. You have been seeking for some extraordinary emotional experience, or some supernatural motivation, or some mystical boldness to share Christ with others. Men of old experienced power in unusual ways, which indeed created boldness to speak out for God.

Perhaps you have compared yourself unfairly with a select group of New Testament Christians. If so, relax. You are not spiritually worthless because you have never had some special "anointing" for witnessing. Remind yourself that God does not demand something from you that you cannot do. But realize that you're a part of a great company of believers, who *together* can share Christ with the world.

God desires that you be able to draw strength and motivation from others in His body. You can be a part of a corporate group of witnessing Christians, making a contribution to His work that is very important in God's sight—no matter what that contribution is. Your very presence, your loving spirit, your service and commitment to others, and your financial support all contribute to God's evangelistic methodology today.

We can all do many specific things to increase "body visibility" before a watching world. But for now, spend a few moments enjoying your salvation. Praise God for what He has done for you. Thank Him that you are an important part of His body, the church, and that in your own way you can contribute your talents or skills. God loves you and values what you do, even if it goes unnoticed by others.

As his custom was, Paul went into the synagogue, and on three Sabbath days he reasoned with them from the Scriptures, explaining and proving that the Christ had to suffer and rise from dead.

Acts. 17:2-3

9

A Total Perspective

In fulfillment of Old Testament prophecies God announced His salvation by sending Jesus Christ, who in Himself was the message of redemption. God also confirmed the Lord's deity by enabling Him to work "signs, wonders and various miracles." The Apostle John illustrated this supernatural methodology and the *results* of this process more dramatically than any of the other Gospel writers. In fact, this is the primary reason why he wrote the history of Christ's life on earth (John 20:30-31). Note how John illustrated this through those who heard Christ teach and saw the miracles He performed.

The Apostles' Message and God's Miracles
We also noted in our previous chapter how this initial evangelistic methodology was carried out by those who heard Christ teach—primarily the apostles. And again, God affirmed this message by giving these men unusual power to work miracles.

The Book of Acts illustrates *how* this power promised in Acts 1:8 was demonstrated and by *whom*, as well as the *results*. The process began with "a sound like the blowing of a violent wind" (Acts 2:2). Those present "saw what seemed to be tongues of fire that separated and came to rest on each of them" (2:3). Next,

THIS SALVATION WAS FIRST ANNOUNCED BY THE LORD . . . . GOD ALSO TESTIFIED TO IT BY SIGNS, WONDERS AND VARIOUS MIRACLES (HEBREWS 2:3-4).

The Message of Salvation Verified by Supernatural Methodology	The People's Response
The Lord changed water to wine (2:1-11)	"He thus revealed his glory, and His disciples put their faith in Him" (2:11b)
The Lord revealed the Samaritan woman's background (4:1-42)	"Many of the Samaritans from that town believed in Him because of the woman's testimony, 'He told me everything I ever did' " (4:39)
The Lord healed the official's son (4:43-54)	"So he [the official] and all his household believed" (4:53b)
The Lord fed the five thousand (6:1-15)	"After the people saw the miraculous sign that Jesus did, they began to say, 'Surely this is the Prophet who is to come into the world' " (6:14)
The Lord walked on the water (6:16-24)	Cumulative response: "We believe and know that you are the Holy One of God" (6:68)
The Lord healed the blind man (9:1-41)	"Then the man said, 'Lord, I believe,' and he worshiped Him" (9:38)
The Lord raised Lazarus from the dead (11:1-45)	"Therefore many of the Jews who had come to visit Mary, and had seen what Jesus did, put their faith in Him" (11:45)

some of those in the group "began to speak in other tongues as the Spirit enabled them" (2:4).

In the midst of this dramatic demonstration of God's power, Peter stood up and preached Christ's death, resurrection, and ascension (2:22-39). Consequently, many believed. In fact, Luke recorded that "about 3,000 were added to their number that day" (2:41). God's phenomenal manifestation of power through these miracles convinced many people that Peter was speaking the truth about Jesus Christ.

The initial supernatural methodology continued to be a part of God's plan to confirm the message of salvation, and wherever God's power was made visible through "signs, wonders and various miracles," many people responded in faith, just as they did when they saw Christ work miracles. Note the following summary from the Book of Acts.

It is clear that as a result of God's miraculous signs done through the apostles and other select New Testament believers, people responded to the message of salvation. Many were convinced that Jesus Christ was indeed the promised Messiah. This fulfilled Christ's promise of power to enable these men to witness of Christ's resurrection. It is also a direct reference to Hebrews 2:3-4.

The Changing Methodology

Beginning in Acts 17 Luke recorded a significant change in God's evangelistic plans. Few miracles are included, though we know they continued to happen. (See Acts 17:1-4; 1 Thes. 1:4; Acts 18:1-11; 1 Cor. 2:4-5; Acts 19:11-12; Gal. 3:5; and Rom. 15:18-19.)

However, beginning in Acts 17 Luke described an added dimension in the methods used by Paul and his traveling companions. There is an emphasis on reasoning, explaining, praising, and examining the Scriptures. In some respects it appears that miracles and signs became less prominent. At least, few miracles are recorded from Acts 17 to the end of Luke's record.

THIS SALVATION...WAS CONFIRMED TO US BY THOSE WHO HEARD HIM. GOD ALSO TESTIFIED TO IT BY SIGNS, WONDERS AND VARIOUS MIRACLES (HEBREWS 2:3-4).

The Message of Salvation Verified by Supernatural Methodology	The People's Response
Peter healed the crippled beggar (3:1-11)	The number of believers grew to about five thousand (4:4)
"The apostles performed many miraculous signs and wonders among the people" (5:12)	"More and more men and women believed in the Lord" (5:14)
Philip performed many wonders and signs (8:6-7)	People "paid close attention to what he said" (8:6) and "accepted the word of God" (8:14)
Peter raised a dead woman (9:40-41)	Many believed (9:42)
Cornelius talked with an angel (10:3) and Peter had a vision (10:9-20)	Cornelius and his household were converted and experienced what the Jews had experienced on the day of Pentecost (10:44-46)
Paul pronounced blindess on Elymas (13:11)	Sergius Paulus believed (13:12)
Paul and Barnabas performed miraculous signs and wonders in Iconium (14:3)	A great number of Jews and Gentiles believed (14:1)
God sent a violent earthquake in Philippi (16:25-26)	The jailer and his household believed (16:34)

THE NATURAL PROCESS OF COMMUNICATION

Methodology	Response
Paul "reasoned with them from the Scriptures, explaining and proving that the Christ had to suffer and rise from the dead" (17:2-3)	"Some of the Jews were persuaded" and "a large number of God-fearing Greeks" and some "prominent women" (17:4)
In Berea they "examined the Scriptures every day" (17:11)	"Many of the Jews believed, as did also a number of prominent Greek women and many Greek men" (17:12)
In Athens Paul "reasoned in the synagogue . . . as well as in the marketplace day by day" (17:17)	"A few men . . . believed" (17:34)
In Corinth Paul "reasoned in the synagogue, trying to persuade Jews and Greeks" (18:4)	"Crispus, the synagogue ruler, and his entire household believed in the Lord; and many of the Corinthians who heard him believed and were baptized" (18:8)

This does not mean that miracles suddenly ceased. They did not, as we've seen from Paul's references to God's power in various epistles which were written to the churches founded after this point in time. Rather, there seems to be a gradual cessation of *supernatural* signs and wonders. These were eventually replaced with the more *natural* process of helping people examine the Scriptures "to see if what Paul said was true" (Acts 17:11). Note the following summary.

As the process of evangelism moved forward in the New Testament world, Christian leaders became more dependent on God's fresh revelation of truth (that is, New Testament doctrine). These doctrines, and the Old Testament Scriptures, were used to confirm the message of salvation. This method of evangelism was more difficult because it took more time. Also, there were fewer recorded conversions.

But this was also part of God's plan. When God launched Israel into prominence as a nation, He did so with great miracles. But once He had revealed His law, and they were established in the land, God put more responsibility on Israel's leaders to keep Israel informed regarding His will.

And when He launched the church at Pentecost, He also gave her great prominence through various signs and wonders. Consequently, thousands were converted to Jesus Christ. But when the church was established, God gradually put more responsibility on people to use His revealed Word, combined with their natural talents and abilities, to communicate the message of salvation.

There seems to be one other reason for this change. Earlier, the apostles ministered primarily to the Jews who lived in the area where Jesus had taught. Many had heard His message numerous times. What the apostles taught when Jesus returned to heaven was not totally new. Consequently, the following words were used to describe their communication process in evangelism: declaring, speaking, teaching, proclaiming, preaching, testifying, witnessing, exhorting and praising. And as the New Testament Christians, particularly the apostles, engaged in this process, God confirmed their message with supernatural events.

But as the apostles moved out from the hub of Jerusalem, they changed their methods. Note the different words that described the communication process: reasoning, refuting, explaining, demonstrating, giving evidence, and persuading.

Most of these people in the outlying regions had heard nothing from Jesus Christ, nor had they heard much about Him. Consequently, the message was new. So Paul had them search the Scriptures to demonstrate that what he was teaching about Jesus Christ was indeed true. However, in many instances God still affirmed this message with miraculous events.

A Third Dimension

The transition in God's evangelistic methodology is not complete until we look carefully at what resulted from God's initial evangelistic strategy—first, the miracles combined with the verbal message; and second, the added process of searching the Scriptures. People were converted in various geographical areas. Local churches came into existence, and the potential for "body visibility" in these locations grew.

This was a new phenomenon. It had existed before only in a limited way through the apostles, who formed the first close-knit group of Christians. At this point, Jesus' command in John 13, His prayer in John 17, and the directives for oneness in the Epistles come into full force. *Unity becomes the final apologetic*.

Today, we are living in this third phase of God's evangelistic methodology. We have the completed Scriptures (God's message) in both the Old and New Testaments. "Miracles, signs, and wonders" as a supernatural means to affirm God's message have ceased as a normal process. (God still has the power to manifest Himself in this way today or at any time in the future.) But we have the potential for love and unity as local bodies never have had before in church history.

God wants to use His Word in believers' lives to empower us. In this way, the Holy Spirit can convince non-Christians that Jesus Christ is God. In this kind of environment, Christ's power and love become a reality to the unbeliever. And it is this miracle—the miracle of love and unity—that God uses today to affirm His salvation message.

Principles for Today

1. Local churches must become dynamic communities of love, reflecting Christ's love for us when He died for us, reflecting His righteous and holy life-style, which He lived out when He walked among men; and reflecting a unity and oneness that illustrates Christ's unity and oneness with the Father.

It is in this context that the message of salvation should and must be taught. It is against this backdrop that personal evangelism becomes very productive and that mass evangelism reaps enduring results. Without this backdrop, the message of salvation, either shared personally or by a speaker to a large group, is often limited to a verbal presentation that has little visual verification. We've seen clearly from Scripture that God intended His message to be affirmed by a dynamic reality—first, by various miracles, followed by the dynamic of Christians who are living in proper relationship to one another.

How can non-Christians be exposed to this kind of Christianity? The church in Jerusalem probably best illustrated how this can happen. They continued in the apostles' teaching and in fellowship all over Jerusalem. They "broke bread in their homes and ate together with glad and sincere hearts." Consequently, they enjoyed "the favor of all the people. And the Lord added to their number daily those who were being saved" (Acts 2:46-47).

Today we frequently wall out non-Christians. They can't "see in." Our present structures often militate against exposing them to love and unity. And because our church meetings are frequently cold and academic, lacking warmth and openness, non-Christians do not feel comfortable coming. And when they do come, we often "preach *at* them" rather than demonstrate love and unity and concern for them and for others in the body of Christ.

Every church should reevaluate its meeting structures. Do they make a non-Christian feel comfortable and welcome? Will this person really see the "body functioning" or will he only see "the preacher or a few other professional" Christian leaders? In the last chapter of this book we'll explore some practical suggestions for changing traditional structures to enable Christians to reflect Christ's love and life-style to unbelievers.

2. Non-Christians should have opportunity to explore the message of the Bible in the context of a loving, nonthreatening community of believers, who in their discussions with one another reflect faith, hope and love—but especially love.

In the early days of Christianity, people most often experienced regeneration and authentic conversion following a rather in-depth exposure to the total message of Christianity. This is best illustrated in the lives of the apostles. To begin with, these men were Jews and already had a basic knowledge of the Old Testament prophecies regarding the coming of their Messiah. In spite of this background, they still had difficulty accepting and believing Christ's message even after having a very close association with the Lord for more than three years, observing His life-style, hearing Him teach and seeing the miracles He performed. But when they did believe His message, their faith was based on a solid foundation and resulted in a dynamic Christian life-style.

The Jews who gathered in Jerusalem for the Feast of Pentecost, and who were converted as a result of Peter's sermon, also illustrate this fact. Many of these people, particularly those from Judea and Galilee, had heard Christ teach many times and had also observed His miracles (Acts 2:22). Like the apostles, their religious heritage was obvious and their faith in Christ was based on both their knowledge of significant prophetic statements and now the fulfillment of those statements.

As the message of Christianity spread rapidly through the geographical areas already touched by Old Testament truth as well as Christ's personal ministry, many people responded to the Gospel. Their previous knowledge combined with the power of the Holy Spirit revealed through the apostles, and others like Philip and Barnabas, resulted in numerous conversions. But as already noted in this chapter, there was a change in evangelistic methodology. As New Testament believers moved out beyond the sphere of devout Judaism and the confines of Christ's earthly ministry, they encountered *both* Jews and Gentiles who knew little of the Old Testament and who had never met Jesus Christ. They knew little, if anything, of what He taught.

It was then that they began to examine the Old Testament Scriptures to see if what they were being taught was indeed true (17:11). This process, combined with confirming miracles, resulted in conversions (1 Thes. 1:4-5). But it is clear from Luke's historical record that this process took more time and the number of conversions decreased considerably compared with what had happened in Jerusalem. Most of those who responded did so on the basis of an exposure to a significant amount of scriptural truth.

Today this process must go on in order to produce conversions. And though God's verifying activity by means of miracles has ceased as a normal process, we can expose non-Christians to another kind of miracle. We can show them a unified body of believers reflecting *faith* in God, *hope* for the present and the future, and *love* for one another and all men. In this way, Jesus said, people would know that He had come from the Father to reveal God's love (John 17:23).

This does not mean that people cannot experience true conversion without a substantial exposure to the total message of Christianity. Many come to Christ through a simple Gospel presentation. However, many who *do* respond to a simple presentation have already been exposed to a great deal of scriptural truth and have observed Christians who have actively lived their faith. In that sense, they are like Timothy who, by learning the Holy Scriptures as a small child, became "wise for salvation through faith in Jesus Christ" (2 Tim. 3:15).

This is perhaps best illustrated at the personal level in the life of the Ethiopian eunuch, a very important public official. He had been to Jerusalem to worship. On the way home, he read from the Book of Isaiah and puzzled over the author's prophetic statements regarding Christ's death. God, through His Spirit, directed Philip to join the Ethiopian and help him understand these Old Testament Scriptures. In the process, Philip led this man to Christ (Acts 8:26-38).

The process and principle, then, are clear from a study of the history of Christianity, both in the New Testament and since New Testament times. The more quality exposure non-Christians have to God's truth as revealed in His Word and as lived out by believers, the more there will be *quality* conversions resulting in growing and spiritually mature Christians.

3. We need Christians today who are uniquely trained and

equipped to engage in confrontation evangelism, and who are able to function in the context of a body of believers who are illustrating the message of Christianity with their lives.

Don't misunderstand. Every believer is responsible to share Christ with others. And it is in the context of "body visibility" that these opportunities come naturally, both when the church as a whole meets to learn, to minister to one another, to worship God, and in small groups. This kind of atmosphere makes it easy to invite non-Christians to share in the experience, thus laying the groundwork for personally communicating the Gospel.

But there is another dimension to personal and group evangelism. Jesus Christ spent three-and-one-half years preparing 11 men to engage in confrontation evangelism and a church planting ministry. Today we need people who are especially prepared to speak publicly to non-Christians. These trained believers should lead Bible studies where non-Christians are present and be able to explain the Scriptures clearly to both believers and unbelievers. Also, they should be able to sensitively answer the difficult questions that many unsaved people are asking today. We need Christians like Peter, John, Philip, Stephen, and Paul—people who are trained to communicate the Gospel and to start churches that can grow into dynamic communities reflecting Christ's love.

In conclusion, it should be noted that starting a new church in a totally pagan culture where there are no other Christians calls for a different strategy. Since most foreign missionaries today do not perform miracles to affirm the Gospel message, they must rely heavily on clear communication of the Scriptures, trusting the Holy Spirit to illuminate minds and hearts to His truth. However, the more this message is taught in a context where its truth can be lived out through relationships with other mature Christians, the greater the impact God's Word will have on the hearts of unbelievers.

Remember that even in New Testament days, Christians seldom engaged in evangelistic efforts alone. Usually, they went out in teams of two or more. Paul exemplified this in his ministry more than any other New Testament evangelist. He always had one or more traveling companions. And *together* they "visualized" the message they taught. (See 1 Thes. 2:1-12 for an example.)

A Personal Response
Get together with several Christians in your church and discuss how you can best apply these principles in your church and community. What can you do personally to encourage this process?

But as for me and my household, we will serve the Lord.
Joshua 24:15

10

Reaching Whole Households

A number of years ago I used these statistics to attempt to prove a point in evangelism strategy. When you try to reach young children for Christ, you get almost a 100 percent response. When you try to reach youth, it may drop to 50 percent. But when you try to reach adults, your chances of winning them drop to almost 0. In other words, it's too late.

Of course, my conclusion seemed obvious. We must concentrate on reaching children and youth if we want success in evangelism. Their hearts are still open, pliable, and ready to respond to the Gospel. And once they become believers, we can mold them into mature Christians.

Then it dawned on me that to draw this conclusion from these statistics was erroneous. Statistics are good, but they can be used to prove almost anything. In this case, my statistics were proving only one thing—performance. Generally speaking, it *was* true that there were fewer decisions for Christ from adults. But to conclude that this *proved* that older people could not be reached was just not true.

We should have concluded that these statistics showed our failure to develop an effective plan for reaching adults—rather than concluding that it was nearly impossible to reach them. Christian history combined with current activity among evangelical Christians proves that we *can* and should be reaching adults for Christ. In fact, this is where we should put our greatest effort and see our greatest results.

When God began His process of reaching the Old Testament world with the Good News that He was the One true God, He began with a grown man—Abraham. When Jesus began His earthly ministry, He began with 12 adults. When the apostles began their ministry in Jerusalem they did not begin with children's meetings, or even youth meetings. They began by reaching adults. But in reaching adults, something very interesting happened. Most often they reached whole households.

Dr. George Peters in his very provocative book entitled *Saturation Evangelism*, states: "Household evangelism and household salvation are the biblical ideal and norm in evangelism and salvation. God wills that the family be one, that it remain a solid and peaceful unit, that the family be evangelized and that the family be saved" (Zondervan, 1970, p. 160).

Two Perspectives

God's ideal plan, beginning in the Old Testament, is that we reach whole households. This is why we read that Noah and his whole household were saved from God's judgment when they as a family entered the ark (Gen. 7:1). And when God called Abraham to leave Ur of the Chaldees, He called his whole family—including his servants—to enter the land of Canaan.

Throughout the rest of the Old Testament we see this pattern, including Joshua who said, "But as for me and my *household*, we will serve the Lord" (Josh. 24:15). Rahab the harlot was one of the most unique examples. She and her whole family were saved from the judgment that fell on Jericho when they believed in the one true God—the God of Abraham, Isaac, and Jacob (6:22-25).

Looking at the New Testament through our own cultural grid, we could conclude that God's plan shifted from an emphasis on groups to an emphasis on individuals. Not so. Rather, household evangelism and conversion is extended into the New Testament era and actually accentuated, through the ministry of Christ and the apostles.

The Ministry of Christ

Jesus exemplified this approach in His own ministry. True, He spoke to the masses and He also dealt with individuals. But generally, it appears that He reached whole households with His divine message.

The nobleman from Capernaum represents an example of household salvation. He went to Cana to meet Jesus and to plead with Him to heal his dying son. While the man was still in Cana, Jesus told him to go home because his son had been healed at that moment. Not only was this a dramatic miracle, but the results were also dramatic in the lives of the nobleman and his family. "He and his whole *household* believed" (John 4:53).

The Ministry of the Apostles

Christ's ministry of household evangelism was only the beginning. The Book of Acts and several of the epistles accentuate household evangelism and conversion. Very early in the history of the church we read that "many who heard the message believed, and the number of men grew to about 5,000" (Acts 4:4). Most Bible expositors believe this is a reference to 5,000 households, just as John wrote that Jesus, during His earthly ministry, fed 5,000 men (John 6:10). Matthew clarified that this was "5,000 men, besides women and children" (Matt. 14:21)— probably a reference to 5,000 households.

Later on in Acts we read about Cornelius' conversion. He was saved along with his whole household, including his relatives and close friends, as a result of Peter's ministry (Acts 10). In Acts 16 Lydia and "the members of her household" became believers and were baptized. And in that same chapter, it was the Philippian jailer's whole family that responded to the Gospel.

Note the references in Acts 16 to the jailer's total family. Following the earthquake that freed the prisoners, "The jailer called for lights, rushed in and fell trembling before Paul and

Silas. He then brought them out and asked, 'Men, what must I do to be saved?' "

"They replied, 'Believe in the Lord Jesus, and you will be saved—you and your *household*.' Then they spoke the word of the Lord to him and to *all the others* in his house. At that hour of the night the jailer took them and washed their wounds; then immediately he and *all his family* were baptized. The jailer brought them into his house and set a meal before them, and the *whole family* was filled with joy, because they had come to believe in God" (16:29-34).

There are other examples in the New Testament. "Crispus, the synagogue ruler, and his entire household believed in the Lord" (Acts 18:8). And later in his first letter to the Corinthian Christians, Paul made reference to the fact that he had baptized the household of Stephanas (1 Cor. 1:16). Paul also refered to the "household of Onesiphorus" when he wrote to Timothy (2 Tim. 1:16). And Philemon and his household represent another dramatic illustration of household evangelism and household salvation.

Observations and Applications

1. The biblical emphasis on "household evangelism" and "household salvation" does not mean families were saved "as a group," but as individuals.

Salvation has always been a matter of personal relationship with God. Even in the Old Testament, not all Israelites were true believers. "A man is not a Jew if he is only one outwardly, nor is circumcision merely outward and physical. No, a man is a Jew if he is one inwardly; and circumcision is circumcision of the heart, by the Spirit, not by the written code" (Rom. 2:28-29).

The same was true in New Testament times. When a household was saved, the members of the households were saved one by one. They may have all been saved at about the same time, but it was a personal experience for every family member. Otherwise, this would contradict the biblical emphasis on personal salvation by faith. Thus, when the Philippian jailer's whole household was saved, it resulted because Paul "spoke the word of the Lord to him [the jailer] and to all the others in his house" (Acts 16:32).

This is important because some people believe a child is saved when he is baptized. Others believe he is saved because of God's covenant with Christian parents. Paul *did* say to the Philippian jailer, "Believe in the Lord Jesus, and you will be saved—you and your household" (16:31). Based on this statement, some Christian parents believe that God has promised to eventually save their children. But this is not an accurate interpretation of what the Bible teaches.

Rather, I believe Paul was referring to those in the household who were old enough to understand the Gospel and respond to it personally by believing in Christ. But God gives no guarantee that very young children will eventually become believers. Though we believe in God's sovereignty and the doctrine of election, we are still responsible to bring up our children "in the training and instruction of the Lord" (Eph. 6:4). If we do not, they may grow up and reject Jesus Christ.

So let's beware. We *should* try to reach whole households. This is a biblical concept. But we must not give the false impression that because the parents become Christians that their children are automatically believers—or will eventually *become* believers because of the parents' commitment. Each of us is responsible before God to respond to the message of salvation. Then and only then are we saved.

2. *Though "household evangelism" and "household conversion" represent a biblical pattern that yields a biblical principle which we can apply today in any situation, cultural factors and dynamics are definitely involved.*

Dr. George Peters spoke to this issue perceptively when he said, "While all people are essentially alike because all are created in the image of God and all have the same qualitative psychological potential, neither the mold nor the configuration of the human soul are the same. The latter two are not essential to man but are the result of the cultural imprint. The mentality of the people can be molded for dictatorship just as it can be formed for democracy. People can be molded for personal responsibility and they can be shaped for social, economic and religious inter-dependence. They can be molded into individualism that recognizes little social interdependence and that little appreciates social relationships. They can also be made into *group people*, bound together by a *group psychology* and thus appreciate *individualism* only to a limited degree" (*Saturation Evangelism*, p. 176).

We must realize that our western mentality is decidedly different than that of those who live in other areas of the world. We have been indoctrinated in individualism, whereas most people in eastern cultures think and act more as a group. To them, the family unit is very important. What the father believes and does often becomes the pattern for the whole family. This was true in biblical days and it is still true in many cultures.

I observed a vivid illustration of this in the lives of a Vietnamese couple who came to the States following the Communist takeover. While on the job, a man in our church led the husband to Christ. When this Vietnamese father came home and shared the experience with his wife, her immediate response was "I'd like to become a Christian too." And she did.

Think for a moment what happens in our culture when a father becomes a Christian. The response from his wife may or may not be positive. Why? Because of our strong cultural emphasis on individualism. Because of this, it is not easy to apply the principle of household evangelism and salvation to families in our western countries.

In fact, it is becoming more and more difficult to reach western families. Many wives have developed an independent spirit that resists being influenced by their husbands' decisions. In school, children are taught to question everything, including their parents' authority.

Nevertheless, the family still exists. Family is a biblical concept that is supracultural. Though modern families are different from families in biblical times, the family unit remains intact, and always will. Likewise, the potential for family conversion still exists.

But today, household conversion depends somewhat on a good relationship between the family members. If a converted spouse follows biblical principles, he often sees dramatic results in his unsaved partner and the other family members. It may take longer in our culture, but often the results *do* eventually come.

The principle of household evangelism is indeed supra-cultural. We see it applied throughout the Bible. It worked among Jews, Gentiles, Greeks, and Romans. We see it applied in Judea, Samaria, and to the uttermost parts of the then known world.

There are no cultural, religious, and geographical limits to this principle. Every local body of believers must find creative ways to use household evangelism in its own culture. We must develop a strategy that will enable us to reach adults—and consequently whole households.

3. While we must recognize other strategies in evangelism, we are wise to put our emphasis where the Bible puts its emphasis.

Household evangelism is not the only model in the Scriptures, although it is one of the predominant ones. And interestingly, it has been the most neglected one, even by foreign missionaries. Most missionaries have been educated in our western culture and are products of an individualistic life philosophy. In fact, most American Christians have been so indoctrinated with individualism that we've tended to overlook the many emphases on corporate experiences in the Bible.

We have personalized almost every biblical directive and exhortation. Consequently, body function and what I prefer to call "body evangelism" have been neglected and replaced almost totally with personal functions—personal Bible study, personal prayer, personal worship, and personal evangelism. Until recently it seems we have not really understood the importance of corporate body function, corporate Christian growth, corporate maturity—*and* corporate evangelism.

But we must be open to all kinds of evangelistic strategies.

Paul said, "I have become all things to all men so that by all possible means I might save some" (1 Cor. 9:22). We must remain free to develop any means that are effective and that do not violate the teachings and principles of Scripture. We need to reach children, youth, and adults—either individually or in groups. We should explore the uses of radio, television, literature, and all other media. At the same time, we should not neglect to use Bible studies, rallies, and crusades. In fact, it is an emphasis on household evangelism by local churches that will make other evangelistic strategies more productive and fruitful, and in some instances, unnecessary.

In conclusion, we should emphasize the approach that brings the best results. Though we cannot say "this method" or "that method" in evangelism is wrong (unless it is in direct violation of some teaching in Scripture), we *can* say this or that method is better or best. Based on Scripture and past results in evangelism, we can without question say that household evangelism represents one of the best—but most neglected—approaches today.

Why is it one of the best? Because it builds dynamic churches. We can never build a strong church on children and youth. We need the maturity of adults—both men and women. And it is from mature Christian families that the church gains its leadership, from elders and deacons who know how to manage their own households. Those who are poor family managers will be poor Christian leaders too (1 Tim. 3:5).

Also a household won to Christ provides a place for nurture. Many young converts (young in physical age) have been lost to Christianity because they had no place to grow spiritually. Unsaved parents either forbade them to go to church or didn't care if they ever went. Consequently, because of childhood immaturity, they never matured spiritually. And if the decision was real, the person became dormant in his Christian experience. If the decision was not real, the positive attitude toward Christ was never nurtured and developed so it eventuated in a true conversion experience.

Finally, household evangelism is a biblical approach. And

whatever the Bible emphasizes as a supracultural principle is one of the best ways to do God's work. We are working in harmony with the Lord Himself.

A Personal and Family Response

A Christian home can become a dynamic "church in miniature" through which love and unity can be demonstrated to non-Christian families. And a household won for Christ can become another "church in miniature" to win other families.

One of the greatest challenges facing the church today is *how* to make the body of Christ visible to unbelievers. Christian homes provide the basic answer, since in most cultures they are spread out geographically among non-Christian family units. Households as corporate units can reach other households for Christ. The various Christian family members can demonstrate to neighbors what Jesus commanded and prayed for in John 13, 15, and 17.

Following is a checklist to help you evaluate the expression of love and unity in your family. Evaluate your present relationship to other family members. Isolate your strengths and weaknesses. Then concentrate on improving your areas of need—to strengthen your family's corporate witness in your neighborhood.

AS A HUSBAND:

	Hardly Ever	A Little	Some	Usually
• I am loving my wife as Christ loved the church (Eph. 5:25).	☐	☐	☐	☐
• I treat my wife as a spiritual equal (Gal. 3:28, 1 Peter 3:7).	☐	☐	☐	☐
• I view my role as a husband as a servant to my wife, just as Christ became a servant to me (Phil. 2:4, 7).	☐	☐	☐	☐
• I demonstrate humility towards my wife, giving up my rights for her happiness and welfare (2:3, 6, 8).	☐	☐	☐	☐
• I am willing to sacrifice my own desires to meet my wife's needs and desires.	☐	☐	☐	☐
• I practice mutual submission with my wife (Eph. 5:21).	☐	☐	☐	☐
• I put forth effort to understand my wife's physical and emotional needs (1 Peter 3:7).	☐	☐	☐	☐

AS A WIFE:

	Hardly Ever	A Little	Some	Usually
• I love my husband as Christ loved me (Eph. 5:1-2).	☐	☐	☐	☐
• I'm learning to love my husband more and more at the feeling level (Titus 2:4).	☐	☐	☐	☐
• I do not lord over my husband, but submit to his authority and love as the church submits to Christ (Eph. 5:22).	☐	☐	☐	☐
• I do all I can to meet my husband's physical and emotional needs (1 Cor. 7:4).	☐	☐	☐	☐
• I attempt to demonstrate a gentle and quiet spirit in our total relationship (1 Peter 3:4).	☐	☐	☐	☐

AS A FATHER & MOTHER:

	Hardly Ever	A Little	Some	Usually
• We are sensitive and gentle towards our children (Col. 3:21).	☐	☐	☐	☐
• We try to understand and meet each individual child's needs (1 Thes. 2:11-12).	☐	☐	☐	☐
• We take our responsibilities seriously to model God's love towards them.	☐	☐	☐	☐
• We fulfill our mutual responsibility to bring them up in the nurture and admonition of the Lord (Eph. 6:4).	☐	☐	☐	☐
• We spend quality time with our children.	☐	☐	☐	☐

AS A CHILD AT HOME:

• I'm obedient to my parents (Eph. 6:1).	☐	☐	☐	☐
• I honor my father and mother (6:2).	☐	☐	☐	☐
• I maintain an open and teachable spirit.	☐	☐	☐	☐
• I respect the rights and privileges of my brothers and sisters.	☐	☐	☐	☐
• I am sincerely trying to be a Christ-like model to my brothers and sisters.	☐	☐	☐	☐

NOTE:

If you are single, living away from home, what can you do to be a part of a "family" outreach and witness to non-Christians?

Always be prepared to give an answer to everyone who asks you to give the reason for the hope that you have.
1 Peter 3:15

11

Five Dimensions of Evangelism

Though we have concentrated in this book on reflecting Christ through corporate and body witness, there are at least five kinds of evangelistic activity in the New Testament. All are essential for a local church to be in the will of God. Though they functionally overlap and are uniquely interrelated, yet they are distinct and recognizable activities. And any 20th-century church that dares to be identified with New Testament principles of evangelism must be involved in all five activities. It is against the backdrop of these biblical functions that we must evaluate our own outreach to the non-Christian world. How does *your* church measure up?

Being
We have observed that what we *are* as a local body of believers is the foundation for an effective witness in our local communities. *Being* what Christ commanded and prayed for in John's Gospel is a dynamic bridge to the world. Our love for one another (John 13:34-35), bearing the fruit of righteousness (15:8), and unity (17:20-23)—all three attract non-Christians, first to us, and then to Jesus Christ. Because of these three qualities, the new Christians in Jerusalem were "enjoying the favor of all the people," resulting in daily conversions (Acts 2:42-47).

117

But this dimension of being is often overlooked when discussing evangelism. Paul and other New Testament writers emphasized the corporate Christian lifestyle because they wanted us to remember its importance. Any church that desires to be in God's will in carrying out the Great Commission must begin in its own "Jerusalem"—creating a community of love, righteousness, and unity that will penetrate the darkness in the minds and hearts of non-Christians.

Going

Though *being* is foundational and essential for effective community outreach, it is only the beginning point. Body visibility only lays the groundwork for personal verbalization. Non-Christians can only understand and comprehend the Gospel as they hear it explained.

New Testament Christians were not ashamed of the Gospel of Jesus Christ. They openly shared their faith with others. As we've seen, certain individuals were more actively involved in direct teaching and preaching, but *all* believers were to be ready to explain why they believed in Jesus Christ. In fact, the New Testament writers assumed that Christians living in the first-century world would find many opportunities to share their faith, simply because of the way they lived. Thus, Peter exhorted, "Always be prapared to give an answer to everyone who asks you to give the reason for the hope that you have" (1 Peter 3:15).

Unfortunately, many of us are never asked this question. This usually means that something is wrong with the way we are living—at least with the way we are viewed by non-Christians. Our "salt" is unavailable. And our "light" is hidden. It cannot penetrate darkness (Matt. 5:13-16). It is God's plan that *wherever* we are, non-Christians should recognize that we have a hope that they don't have. After they realize this, often they will feel free to ask why (Col. 4:5-6).

Sending

All Christians are not called to leave their homes and communities in order to be evangelists and missionaries. In fact, most of the New Testament converts never left their pagan communities. Rather, they remained where they were and became a dynamic corporate and personal witness to their neighbors.

But some *did* experience both the call of God and the call of men to present the message of Christ in other areas of the world. The apostles stand out as Christ's primary ambassadors in carrying out the Great Commission. They were His first followers. And they were His first evangelists.

But many others also became involved in world evangelization. In fact, Luke recorded that when severe religious persecution hit Jerusalem, "All except the apostles were scattered throughout Judea and Samaria." And, "those who had been scattered preached the Word wherever they went" (Acts 8:1-4).

Eventually, however, persecution subsided. The "church throughout Judea, Galilee and Samaria enjoyed a time of peace. It was strengthened; and encouraged by the Holy Spirit, it grew in numbers, living in the fear of the Lord" (9:31).

Eventually this persecution ceased to be a prime motivator in scattering Christians to other locations. Then the local churches that were founded during this persecution continued to send evangelists to other locations. For example, the church at Antioch first commissioned Saul and Barnabas as missionaries (13:3). On another occasion the church in Jerusalem selected Judas and Silas to minister in Antioch (15:22-33). And Paul influenced Timothy to leave his friends and family and join him in evangelistic work (16:1-3).

In Corinth, Paul met Aquila and Priscilla. When Paul left this city later, this husband and wife team decided to join him in his work. Thus we read that Paul left Corinth and "sailed for Syria, accompanied by Priscilla and Aquila" (18:18).

When this evangelistic team arrived at Ephesus, Aquila and Priscilla remained behind while Paul went on to Caesarea. At that point, this couple met a brilliant and dynamic speaker named Apollos. He was very knowledgeable in the Old Testament Scriptures but lacked understanding regarding New Testament doctrine (18:24-25). Aquila and Priscilla personally taught Apollos the full truth in Jesus Christ (18:26).

This additional knowledge of God's Word evidently instilled in Apollos an even greater desire to minister to others. Consequently, he went to Achaia. We read that "The brothers encouraged him and wrote to the disciples there to welcome him" (18:27).

The process is clear. In the initial days of New Testament Christianity certain people carried the Gospel as a result of a direct call and command of Jesus Christ. But God gradually ceased to speak directly to people. Then the process whereby individuals decided to become evangelists did not result from a direct call from God, but from an exposure to the Gospel, a knowledge of God's will through His revealed Word, and other missionary models.

Through their own experiences with Christ and through the efforts of others, these believers became burdened to share the Lord with unbelievers. And in each case, various groups of believers sent out other believers to help carry out the Great Commission in areas beyond their immediate communities.

Giving

Financially supporting those who have a desire to serve Jesus Christ as full-time evangelists and missionaries is just as much a part of carrying out the Great Commission as *going*. From a Christian viewpoint, we cannot conscientiously send people out without meeting their physical and financial needs.

This is a principle established early in religious history. God commanded Israel to give one-tenth of all their material resources to meet the physical needs of the Levites. These individuals were set apart by God to care for the tabernacle. Consequently, they were not assigned a portion of land when they came into Canaan. Their material needs were to be met by others in Israel (Num. 18:21-24).

Jesus reiterated this principle in His New Testament discourses (Matt. 10:10; Luke 10:7). Later, Paul quoted Jesus in his letter to

Timothy. Here he emphasized that elders who direct church affairs should be remunerated for their efforts (1 Tim. 5:17). "For the Scripture says, 'Do not muzzle the ox while it is treading out the grain,' and 'The worker deserves his wages' " (1 Tim. 5:18; see also 1 Cor. 9:7-21).

The Philippian church was a unique example of believers supporting those who preached the Gospel. And Paul, their spiritual father, was their primary concern. In fact, it was their gift to Paul that prompted him to write the Philippian Epistle. "I rejoice greatly in the Lord," he said, "that at last you have renewed your concern for me" (Phil. 4:10). And later Paul commended them for being the first church in Macedonia to care for his physical needs (4:14-16).

But what is a New Testament perspective on giving? What principles should guide us in our giving? Some say it should be the Old Testament tithe; that is, 10 percent. However, we should realize that every year the children of Israel gave 20 percent—10 percent to the Levites and 10 percent to be set aside for a special celebration in Jerusalem (Deut. 12:5-6, 11, 18). In addition, every third year an additional 10 percent was collected to care for strangers, the fatherless, widows, and any additional needs the Levites might have (26:12-15; 14:28-29). The average annual total was approximately 23 percent of their yearly income.

If the Old Testament is to guide us, Christians should at least be giving two tithes, plus a third tithe every third year. The fact is, the New Testament does not spell out how much Christians should give to the Lord's work. Rather, the Scriptures lay down several principles to guide us.

1. We are to give systematically. When writing to the Corinthians, Paul instructed them to set aside a sum of money "on the first day of every week" (1 Cor. 16:2). Obviously, there were cultural factors involved in this pattern, but the principle is clear. Though Christians in our culture may be paid every two weeks, or monthly, or even in some instances yearly, they are to set aside a certain amount regularly to give to God's work. Christians are to give systematically. It is not to be haphazard. It is to be planned just as carefully as any other item in our budgets.

2. *We are to give proportionately.* In the same verse Paul instructed the Corinthians to give "in keeping with their income." If they made much, they were to give much. If they did not make much, they were to give less. But they were *all* to give, no matter how small or large their income.

This is a unique principle. It goes beyond the first, second, or even third tithe in the Old Testament. Some Christians are able to give 50 percent and still have plenty to meet their own needs, whereas other Christians may give less than one-tenth because of their incomes. Paul's principle allows for both situations.

I suggest that every Christian begin his giving program with at least 10 percent of his income, trusting God to meet his needs. My wife and I did this from the beginning of our marriage, even though our income was minimal and it took many years to acquire household furnishings that were beyond bare necessities. God has honored that in our lives, enabling us to have some of those things now. He has even made it possible for us to increase our giving beyond 10 percent.

I know of a Christian businessman in Chicago who has given 30 percent of his income to the Lord ever since he's been in business. And he has never lacked. In fact, he has lived very well. And most of us have heard of the late R. G. LeTourneau, the designer and developer of the great earthmoving equipment that is used around the world. Mr. LeTourneau placed 90 percent of the stock of his company in a foundation committed to the Lord's work.

3. *We are to give cheerfully.* In Paul's second letter to the Corinthians, he laid down a third principle. "Remember this: Whoever sows sparingly will also reap sparingly, and whoever sows generously will also reap generously. Each man should give what he has decided in his heart to give, not reluctantly or under compulsion, for God loves a cheerful giver" (2 Cor. 9:6-7).

God is not pleased if we give reluctantly and under compulsion. This is the principle of grace. Freely we have received, and freely we are to give. This is true worship. And this is true gratitude for what God has given to us in Jesus Christ.

4. When we live according to God's principles we can expect God to meet our needs. Following Paul's instructions to give generously and cheerfully, he also wrote: "God is able to make all grace abound to you, so that in all things at all times, having met all that you need, you will abound in every good work" (9:8).

It's important to note that God has not promised to *multiply* our income if we give. But He has promised to meet our needs. In some instances, the Lord pours out unusual blessings on Christians—both financially and spiritually.

How much then should a Christian give? The Bible doesn't say. Rather, we are to give systematically, proportionately, and cheerfully, expecting that we cannot outgive God. He will not let us down, though He may test our motives to see if we are truly giving out of a heart of love.

When Christians give according to these principles, there will be plenty of money to support God's work. Indeed, we are under obligation to take care of those who labor in the gospel.

Praying

Last, but not least, is the evangelistic activity called prayer. Christians are to feel free to pray about many things—in fact, about *all* things (Phil. 4:6). But there are specific New Testament examples to demonstrate how important prayer is for those laboring in the Gospel. Paul knew he could not adequately fulfill his missionary responsibilities without prayer support. Consequently, he wrote to the Colossians: "Devote yourselves to prayer, being watchful and thankful. And pray for us too that God may open a door for our message, so that we may proclaim the mystery of Christ, for which I am in chains. Pray that I may proclaim it clearly, as I should" (Col. 4:2-4).

Here Paul asked for prayer so that he might have an opportunity to speak for Christ. But secondly, he requested prayer so that he might communicate the message of Christ clearly.

When writing to the Romans he requested prayer that he might be protected from his enemies in Jerusalem, and also that he might be accepted by Christians who could have misinterpreted his ministry (Rom. 15:30-31). And when writing to the Corinthians he requested prayer for deliverance from hardship and severe pressures (2 Cor. 1:8-11).

Paul also requested prayer from the Philippians for deliverance (Phil. 1:19)—not so much deliverance from prison and pressure, but that he might not be ashamed of Christ when he stood before the emperor of Rome. "I eagerly expect and hope that I will in no way be ashamed, but will have sufficient courage so that now as always Christ will be exalted in my body, whether by life or by death" (1:20).

Obviously, those who are involved in evangelism need prayer—prayer for open doors, for liberty in speaking, for protection, for deliverance, and for boldness. Local bodies of believers are responsible to pray regularly for their members who are "out on the front lines." Christians who pray are just as involved in carrying out the Great Commission as those who share the Gospel.

A Personal Response
Scripture shows that many New Testament evangelists, including Paul, expected Christ to return within their lifetime. Actually, they seemed to believe that they had carried the Gospel to the whole world. Obviously, they were limited in their knowledge, both in terms of space and time. And, of course, this was by God's design. For as Jesus said, "The Son of Man will come at an hour when you do not expect Him" (Matt. 24:44).

Today we know that Christ did not return in the first century, and He has still not come—and it's been nearly 2,000 years. And we also know from the perspective of Scripture that He has not returned because it is His desire that no one be lost (2 Peter 3:9). And we also know that these five dimensions of evangelistic activity are just as relevant today as they were in the first century.

Following are a series of questions related to the five

dimensions of evangelistic activity presented in this chapter, with a place to write a personal goal for each area. Every Christian should set goals in all five areas.

Read the questions in each area. Write out a personal goal for each area. Number each goal from 1 to 5 reflecting a priority sequence for reaching each goal. NOTE: *Determine your priorities in terms of the greatest need in your life to be obedient to God's Word. All five dimensions are important if we are to be in God's will.*

1. What are you doing (or not doing) as an individual to contribute to the love, righteousness, and unity that Christ prayed for in order that your immediate family and local church might be a dynamic witness in the world? What can you do immediately?

Personal Goal: _____

2. What are you doing to share your faith with others—with your neighbors, with those you work with, your friends? Do these people even know that you are a Christian? Is your life attractive to them? Do they know what your hope really is? If not, what can you do that you are not doing in order to communicate these facts?

Personal Goal: _____

3. What are you doing to encourage others to serve Jesus Christ? Have you ever considered the possibility of serving Jesus Christ full-time yourself—especially in another part of the world?

Personal Goal: _____

NOTE: *Though the apostles and prophets were uniquely called and gifted to lay the foundation of the church in the first century, we need to follow their example by sending forth missionaries to function basically in the same role. Today we need men and women who can plant churches, especially in places where the name of Christ has not been heard. Is there any reason why you should not consider the possibility?*

4. What are you doing to support your church financially? Are you giving systematically, proportionately, and cheerfully?

Personal Goal:_____

5. What are you doing to support evangelists and missionaries in prayer, including your own pastoral staff? What can you do that you are not now doing?

Personal Goal: _____

Speak to one another with psalms, hymns and spiritual songs. Sing and make music in your heart to the Lord, always giving thanks to God the Father for everything, in the name of our Lord Jesus Christ.

Ephesians 5:19-20

12

Moving from Principles to Patterns

In this study we've attempted to search deeply into Scripture for basic principles of evangelism that emerge as supracultural guidelines for us. Once these principles become sharply focused in our thinking, we're then responsible to apply them creatively in our own culture. We must move from functions to form; from principles to patterns; from message to methodology.

The major emphasis of this book has been corporate or body evangelism. You have had opportunity to personally apply these principles at the conclusion of each chapter. But beyond this it is absolutely essential—in order to be true to these principles—to think specifically how you can apply these principles *corporately*.

Though *being* is only one of five major emphases of New Testament evangelism, it *is* foundational and has been virtually overlooked, both in the past and in the present. And because there are numerous books that emphasize practical ways to share Christ personally, this chapter will focus on practical suggestions for making disciples through *being disciples*. Hopefully, you'll find something that can be applied to your life.

But first, let's review. Following are the major principles that have emerged from our study and which focus on corporate witness.

1. Every local church (wherever Christians meet regularly for edification) must become a dynamic community:

   a. Reflecting Christ's love that motivated Him to die for us
   b. Reflecting His righteous and holy life-style, which He lived out when He walked among men, and
   c. Reflecting a unity and oneness that illustrates Christ's unity and oneness with the Father.

2. Non-Christians should have opportunity to explore the message of the Bible in the context of this loving, non-threatening community of believers, who in their discussions and interactions with one another reflect both "faith, hope and love"—but especially love. It is in this context that the written Word of God becomes living and dynamic since it is being manifested through believers in their relationships with one another.

3. We need Christians today who are uniquely trained and equipped to engage in confrontation evangelism, and who are able to function in a context of a body of believers who are illustrating the message of Christianity with their lives. This kind of community provides a backdrop against which Christianity appears logical and realistic, and it serves as a means to bring unbelievers to faith in Christ. Put another way, true Christianity as it's lived out through Christians, serves as a dynamic means to sensitively counter the objections that people have regarding historic Christianity and its claim to be the one true religion.

4. Though we must use every legitimate means to communicate the Gospel to non-Christians, we should concentrate our efforts on reaching adults and, consequently, whole families for Christ. It is this approach which builds strong churches and in turn sets in motion the process whereby the principles just stated can be effectively worked out and applied in the twentieth-century world.

The Church Building

Inherent in the concept of corporate evangelism is the necessity for Christians to meet together and to function as a loving, unified body. If non-Christians are to see and experience Christ's love reflected and lived through Christians who love one another, we *must* assemble together regularly for this to actually happen. In fact, the word *church* (ekklesia) actually means an "assembly." Historically and biblically it does not refer to a building, although we often use the word in this way.

Before discussing the church building as a place for body evangelism to take place, we must clarify one important issue. It is true that the Christians in Jerusalem met "from house to house" (Acts 5:42) because they had no permanent place to meet as a group. Furthermore, their numbers increased so rapidly that there was no building large enough to hold them, even if they had met in a permanent facility. To complicate matters, the Jewish temple soon became "off limits" because of a serious theological rift between the Jews who believed that Jesus Christ was the true Messiah and those who did not.

This lack of permanent meeting facilities continued to be a problem for Christians in the New Testament culture for years. In fact, one of the first buildings used primarily as a regular place for Christian meetings has been discovered by archaeologists in the ruins of the ancient city Dura-Europus in the Syrian desert. It was originally used as a private home by a well-to-do person. The date of construction was the year A.D. 232-233. (Jack Finegan, *Light from the Ancient Past*, Vol. 2. Princeton University Press, 1946, pp. 495-499.) In others words, this indicates that when it became a possibility, Christians used church buildings, even though they had to adapt homes for this purpose. But we must recognize that this happened many years after the events recorded in the New Testament.

Several of us in Dallas experimented with the house church idea for several months before launching Fellowship Bible Church in a permanent facility. The house church grew slowly over a period of six months, and provided many meaningful experiences for those involved. But when we launched the work in a permanent facility, the difference in interest, commitment, and numerical growth was almost incredible. And since then we have launched a number of branch churches and have observed the same phenomena. The more permanent the facility, the more rapid the growth, both quantitatively and qualitatively.

Generally speaking, why don't 20th-century people (Americans particularly) respond to the "house church"? The reasons are primarily cultural and psychological. Many people do not feel you are taking church seriously unless you meet in a permanent facility. They seem to need the security of a church building, which is understandable when you take into consideration the mind-set of people today, particularly those of us who live in the western sector of the world.

It must also be pointed out that early Christians sacrificed several unique qualities when they moved from houses to church buildings. They began to lose the intimacy of smaller groups, the emotional warmth of the home environment, and the "family" climate created there. And this leads us to some very practical suggestions.

Environment and Communication Styles

When using church buildings there are ways we can apply the love, life-style, and unity principle in our contemporary culture. First, the building can be designed to reflect the informality, warmth and relaxed atmosphere of a home. Soft chairs can replace pews and floors can be carpeted. Pulpits can be removed so they will not become an obstruction between pastors and people. Also, platforms can be designed so that church leaders do not appear to be "above" the people.

Even in a traditional setting, the very atmosphere of the church building can reflect warmth and informality. This depends somewhat on the attitudes of church leaders. Those directing a church service should not put on a false air of formality. Rather, they should display the same kind of attitude they would show toward guests in their own homes.

When I first became involved in our ministry in Dallas, I found it difficult to practice these principles. For years, I had been culturally conditioned to change my behavior once I mounted the platform to teach and preach. Like many, I equated "being formal" with being reverent and spiritual.

Then I imagined I was sitting at home sharing biblical thoughts and ideas with my guests who were sitting around me. I found it helpful, at least initially, to sit as I taught and preached. (Incidentally, if you had guests in your home and you were sharing a biblical message with them, you wouldn't lean forward, point your finger, pound the coffee table, and shout.)

If the church service is structured so as to create a home atmosphere, it encourages believers to invite non-Christians. In this way, they can experience the realities of Christianity as they are reflected through a loving and unified local body of Christians. It is in this context that the Holy Spirit has full opportunity to convince non-Christians of their need for Jesus Christ. True, He always honors the Word of God. But it is when the Word is lived out in Christlike relationships that the environment provides maximum potential for effective communication with unbelievers.

Making the Gospel Clear

A word needs to be said about the traditional evangelistic sermon and invitation in some traditional churches. Obviously, this approach is still effective in some cultural settings. But many people do not respond to this approach as they once did. Again, the reasons are cultural and psychological. Our contemporary society has moved from a very excited type of communication into a more calm style. This is true in both both radio and television communication.

Several years ago "staccato" and "rapid-fire" methods of broadcasting were popular. Today the approach is much more low-key. Talk shows have conditioned people to "listen in on" rather than to be "talked at." And there is a general negative reaction to high-pressure tactics and methods. Modern commercials and advertising campaigns must be far more subtle and indirect to get people to listen and to respond.

As Christians we cannot ignore these general social and

psychological changes in people. Pastors who continue to preach *at* non-Christians often create negative reactions that result in rejection of the Gospel rather than acceptance. People often feel talked down to and emotionally rejected.

The issue here is not our theology, but our methodology. True, non-Christians *are* lost in sin and must be told so without equivocation. However, we must speak a "language" they understand. And when the body of Christ functions as it should, reflecting Christ's love, His life-style, and His unity, unbelievers sense an overwhelming impact.

In our own ministry, we have seen many people ask Christ into their lives as they were assembled with the body of Christ. Furthermore, it is very natural to invite people to receive Christ as their Saviour without putting them under pressure, embarrassing them, and creating a negative reaction.

In our churches we have also overlooked the impact clear Bible teaching has on non-Christians. Many unbelievers are very interested in knowing what the Bible actually says and means. And when it is taught clearly, objectively, and lovingly—and in a context of an accepting community of believers—the Holy Spirit uses God's truth to convince unbelievers of their spiritual need. Furthermore, they grasp the Gospel message in the context of the total message of Christianity. Again, this approach leads to qualitative decisions for Christ.

Body Function

In the average church, services are structured so that only a few people participate. The primary person, and in some churches the only person who is visible, is the pastor. The majority of Christians attending the service, aside from participating in congregational singing and the offering, sit and listen to one man teach.

Though this kind of service *can* be designed to create a warm and accepting atmosphere, it does not really allow non-Christians to *see* Christians express love and concern for others. There may indeed be love and unity in the church, but it is not visible.

The visibility of love was a basic ingredient in the Jerusalem church that caused many non-Christians to be "added to their number daily" (Acts 2:47). Not only were non-Christians exposed to the apostles' teaching (the Word of God), but they also saw other members honoring the Lord through the communion meal. They saw believers praying for one another and sharing their material possessions with those in need.

And they saw and heard these Christians "praise God"—as they no doubt taught one another with psalms, hymns, and spiritual songs (Eph. 5:19-20). Through these dynamic relationships with one another, the early Christians enjoyed "the favor of all the people"—obviously the non-Christians in Jerusalem (Acts 2:47).

The point of application is clear. Church services today *must* be structured, not only for the pastor to teach the Word of God, but for the body of Christ to function.

When we started our work in Dallas in 1972, we tried to design a service that enabled the body of Christ to function along with good Bible teaching. Consequently, we structured our service with three basic components—a basic hour for teaching, about 20 minutes for coffee and fellowship, and another hour for sharing and body participation (see Figure 6). We called this second hour our "fellowship and sharing service."

Some call this kind of service an "open meeting" or a "body life" service. In our particular situation, the fellowship and sharing service usually followed the teaching and preaching hour, thus giving people opportunity to share in the light of a fresh encounter with the Word of God.

Periodically we would reverse the format and begin with the sharing hour, followed by the teaching hour. Both approaches worked well. However, exposing people to the Word of God first helped to relate the sharing more specifically to the Scriptures. We felt this was a decided advantage and consequently we usually began with the teaching hour.

For an extended period of time (about six years) this was our format—one that worked very effectively. However, after six

2¼ HOUR STRUCTURE

Preparation
(Primarily Music)

BIBLE
TEACHING
1. Exposition
2. Application
3. Life Response

Introduce Visitors

Coffee Break

FELLOWSHIP
and
SHARING
(Body Function)

Invitation and Offering

FELLOWSHIP
and
SHARING

Introduce Visitors

Coffee Break

Preparation (Music)

BIBLE
TEACHING

Invitation and Offering

years of experience and evaluation, we decided to change. We combined the teaching and sharing elements into a 90-minute service with a 15-minute coffee break at the end. In some respects we feel it has been an improvement over our original format. Primarily, it gives us more flexibility and balance within a solid time block (see Figure 7 for illustrations of this flexibility).

This flexibility involves:

1. Natural opportunities for questions and comments immediately following the message.

2. Natural opportunities to respond in worship to the message, without a break in continuity (some messages lend themselves more to worship; some messages lend themselves to questions and discussion; some messages lend themselves to body ministry).

3. More flexibility with music throughout the service.

4. More flexibility with the various elements as illustrated in figure 7.

Meetings in Homes

In New Testament days, house churches involved what is often called the "extended family." In addition to fathers and mothers, brothers and sisters, there were grandparents, aunts, uncles, cousins—and servants. In fact, in many instances whole households came to Christ, forming the nucleus for a local church.

In our western culture, this is a foreign concept. But from another perspective, we can form our own "extended families" for reaching others for Christ. In addition to creating an atmosphere of warmth and acceptance with a church building, we should schedule meetings in private homes. This makes it easier for non-Christians to attend and to see Christians interacting with one another as caring and sharing people.

Since these are neighborhood meetings, unbelievers probably will feel less threatened and more relaxed than they would in a structured church service. In this way, Christians can meet from

Music and Sharing
BIBLE TEACHING
LIFE RESPONSE (Body Function)
Introduce Visitors
Coffee Time

Preparation
BIBLE TEACHING
Questions and Comments on Message
SHARING (Body Function)
Introduce Visitors
Coffee Time

Preparation
BIBLE TEACHING
Worship Music
SHARING
Introduce Visitors
Coffee Time

house to house just as New Testament Christians did. But they still have a permanent place (a church building) for larger meetings. Furthermore, meetings in homes encourage non-Christians to eventually participate in the larger, more structured church service.

Bible Studies. Home Bible studies are perhaps the greatest untapped means for engaging in "body evangelism." Unfortunately, we have often advocated believers' Bible studies (for Christians only) or, on the other hand, we have emphasized the need for evangelistic home Bible studies—those designed primarily for non-Christians. But we need a combination of these two approaches.

Some studies can be structured and led by different members of the group, including non-Christians. These are more discussion type studies. Each person, utilizing a study guide, takes his turn in leading the Bible discussion. In this way, non-Christians are treated as members of the group. And in studying the Bible to prepare to lead the study, many people become Christians.

Other Bible studies should be directed by leaders with training in basic Bible content and teaching methods. These are more expositional studies, with appropriate group interaction, involving questions and answers, comments and personal opinions. Leaders should be sensitive, gentle, and patient. In this kind of Bible study, the leader's own attitude will set the stage for interaction among the group members. And again, this provides a context for non-Christians to be exposed to the Word of God in a loving and accepting community of believers.

Special Parties. Another very effective "bridge building" technique is to conduct a special party—at Christmastime, on or near Valentine's Day, or during the Easter season. A Mother's Day or Father's Day party for all the mothers or fathers in the neighborhood is also a unique time to communicate with non-Christians.

All of these events provide unusual opportunities to focus on God's love—and in nonthreatening ways. Invitations should refer to the fact that the party will also have a spiritual emphasis. Thus, non-Christians do not feel manipulated into attending a "religious" meeting without knowing it.

Film Presentations. I was personally involved in coordinating a concentrated effort in various homes in Dallas using a series of films about Christianity and science. We used the films produced by Moody Institute of Science and showed them in different homes each evening during the week.

In our own home we followed each film with refreshments and a time for natural response. There was no planned discussion, but by the end of the fourth film, people began to ask specific questions about the Bible. As a result of these discussion times, one home Bible study was organized and several people were converted.

There are other film series that can be used in the same way—films on prophecy, the family, culture, and many other subjects. With this approach, it is important to respond to questions and comments tactfully, with wisdom and insight. Though disagreements may arise, a mature and informed Christian leader can help maintain an unusual spirit of acceptance and love in the group.

However, the group leader must be able to teach as defined in 2 Timothy 2:24-26: "And the Lord's servant must not quarrel; instead, he must be kind to everyone, able to teach, not resentful. Those who oppose him he must gently insruct, in the hope that God will grant them a repentance leading them to a knowledge of the truth, and that they will come to their senses and escape from the trap of the devil, who has taken them captive to do his will."

The Home—The Church in Miniature

The Christian family itself, when functioning according to God's guidelines, is the most basic unit for engaging in corporate evangelism. In God's scheme, it represents the church in miniature. And since the purpose of every local church is to reveal God's glory to all men, that purpose extends into every Christian home.

How does a home come to be a vibrant testimony in the

community? This happens when members of each family follow and practice God's guidelines recorded in Ephesians 5:22—6:4:
- wives submit to their husbands as to the Lord
- husbands love their wives as Christ loved the church
- children respect, honor, and obey their parents in the Lord
- fathers raise their children in the training and instruction of the Lord

This process produces unity and oneness—a demonstration of Christlikeness which becomes the dynamic bridge to reach non-Christian neighbors—a bridge over which we can walk to share the direct message of the Gospel and to lead other families to Jesus Christ.

But this love, life-style, and unity must be *seen* by non-Christians if it is to function as a bridge. This is why there is so much emphasis in the New Testament on hospitality. Christians *should* invite non-Christians into their homes to experience this reality. For example, inviting another family over for dinner, and then graciously asking them to join you in giving thanks for the food, makes an impact that is seldom forgotten. And when done properly, it is not threatening to your guests. Often this opens the door for conversations about spiritual issues.

Remember that times spent with non-Christian families should be natural. Do what you would normally do—play games, watch a sports event on television, or chat about the day's activities. Don't put on airs. Relax—be yourself. Just reflect the love of Christ in all that you do.

Opportunities for Christian witness grow naturally out of these times together. It may happen some day when wives are together for coffee, when husbands meet outside mowing their lawns, or when children are playing together.

Taking the Gospel to the World

In our culture, sometimes it is wise to use neutral facilities to conduct evangelistic meetings. People who would never darken the door of a church will attend a meeting held in a school auditorium, a stadium, or a clubhouse. This is particularly important when various churches and denominations cooperate in an evangelistic effort.

This strategy is well-known in our contemporary environment. There are problems, however. It is often difficult to interest non-Christians in attending these crusades and meetings. People suspect that they are being led into something they'd rather avoid. Consequently, many times these crusades turn into revival meetings for Christians, primarily because very few non-Christians are present. There are some notable exceptions, such as the Billy Graham Crusades.

But what can be done to reach people for Christ in a smaller setting? Some significant changes need to be made in our approach. High pressure tactics need to be eliminated. Fundraising efforts in the meetings themselves should be avoided so that non-Christians do not misinterpret motives. Leaders should try to create an atmosphere of warmth, acceptance, and oneness among those Christians who attend.

Also, preaching style should be culturally adapted. Evangelistic sermons must contain significant biblical content—interestingly delivered, but true to the text and context of the Bible. Manipulative techniques should be avoided. And the whole climate should convey concern, reality, honesty, integrity, and pure motives. In short, the body of Christ should be visible in meetings of this nature, with as much audience participation as possible.

A Corporate Life Response

So far, our response projects have been personal, basically because our personal attitudes and actions are involved if we are to be mature, functioning members of Christ's body. However, this final project is corporate. To correctly apply the biblical principles outlined here requires a group response. The following steps will give you specific suggestions on how your church might proceed to develop a more effective corporate witness.

Step 1. If you have read this book on your on, make plans to study it together with a larger group of Christians—in a Sunday

School class, in a home Bible study, or in some other study group. If you are a pastor, you may wish to preach a series of sermons on the theme, "Loving One Another."

Step 2. To help the church focus on "body evangelism," the church's governing board should follow up the pastor's series on corporate evangelism with some serious discussion. Church leaders should explore how they can create an open environment in their church services. In this way, members can demonstrate love and unity to visitors. This may mean changing the service structure and format to allow more opportunity for interaction.

Step 3. Someone should be appointed in the church (preferably a staff person who can give quality time) to organize and administer a program of home Bible studies. These studies should be designed to reach unbelievers by demonstrating the realities of Christianity in the context of biblical truth.

Step 4. These home studies can be supplemented with special neighborhood parties and film showings. Again, this will take careful coordination and planning.

Step 5. Church families should be challenged to use their homes to demonstrate hospitality and love to their non-Christian neighbors.

Step 6. Encourage families in a particular community to consider planning events in a neutral neighborhood facility. In this way, they can develop relationships with non-Christians and present the Gospel.